Wood Pellet Smoker and Grill Cookbook

The Ultimate Barbecue Cookbook for Smoking and Grilling Irresistible Meat, Poultry, Fish, Vegetable, Game Recipes

D1716403

By Adam Jones

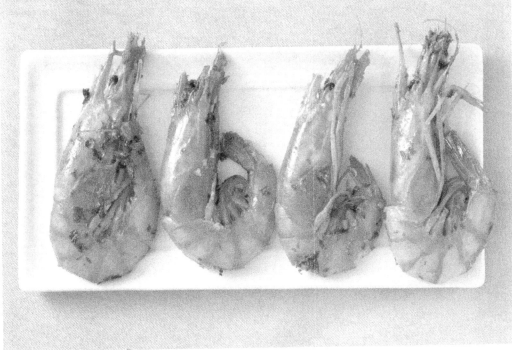

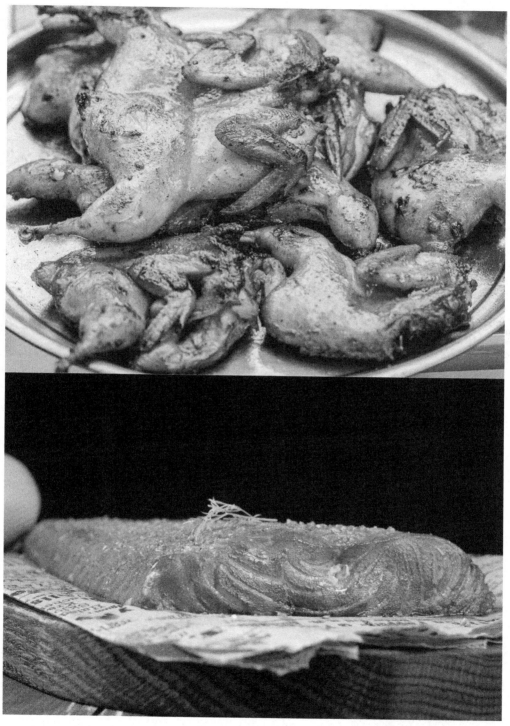

TABLE OF CONTENTS

7

INTRODUCTION

Wood pellet smokers very easily provide the option to smoke meats through an easy-to-use and accessible interface. Where there is a smoke, there is a flavor. Smoking meat or making BBQ is not only a means of cooking but for some individuals and classy enthusiasts, this is a form of Art! Or dare I say a form of lifestyle! Enthusiasts all around the world have been experimenting and dissecting the secrets of perfectly smoked meat for decades now, and in our golden age, perhaps they have cracked it up completely! In our age, the technique of Barbequing or Smoking meat has been perfected to such a level, that a BBQ Grill is pretty much an essential amenity found in all backyard or sea-beach parties!

This is the drinking fountain for the more hip and adventurous people, who prefer to have a nice chat with their friends and families while smoking up a few batches of Burger Patty for them to enjoy. But here's the thing, while this art might seem as a very easy form of cooking which only requires you to flip meats over and over! Mastering it might be a little bit difficult if you don't know have the proper information with you. This guide is an essential book for beginners who want to smoke meat without needing expert help from others. This book offers detailed guidance obtained by years of smoking meat, includes clear instructions and step-by-step directions for every recipe. This is the only guide you will ever need to professionally smoke a variety of food. The book includes photographs of every finished meal to make your job easier. Whether you are a beginner meat smoker or looking to go beyond the basics, the book gives you the tools and tips you need to start that perfectly smoked meat. Smoking is something has withstood the test of time, it will continue to stand the test of time for years to come. Not only is it a method to preserve your catch or kill, but it's also one of if not the best-tasting food there is.

CHAPTER-1 PORK
CHIPOTLE AND BLACKBERRY GLAZE SMOKED PORK BUTT WITH CITRUS AROMA

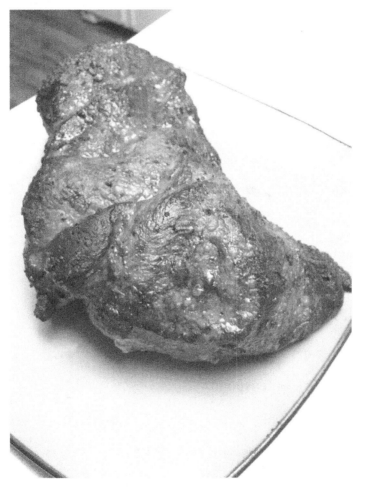

(COOKING TIME 6 HOURS 10 MINUTES)

INGREDIENTS FOR 10 SERVINGS

- Pork butt (4-lbs., 1.8-kg.)

THE MARINADE

- Unsweetened orange juice - ¾ cup
- Lemon juice - 2 tablespoons
- Olive oil - 1 ½ tablespoon
- Chopped bay leaves - 1 tablespoon
- Minced garlic - 2 teaspoons
- Red chili flakes - 1 teaspoon
- Black pepper - 1 teaspoon

THE GLAZE

- Fresh blackberries - 2 cups
- Blackberry jam - 3 tablespoons
- Chopped chipotle pepper - 2 tablespoons
- Apple cider vinegar - 3 tablespoons
- Orange zest - 1 tablespoon
- Salt - ¼ teaspoon
- Black pepper - ¼ teaspoon

THE SPRAY

- Apple cider vinegar - 1 cup

THE HEAT

- Cherry wood pellet

METHOD

1. Pour orange juice, lemon juice, and olive oil into a container. Stir until incorporated.

2. Season the mixture with bay leaves, minced garlic, red chili flakes, and blackberries. Mix well.

3. Score the pork butt at several places and put it into the marinade mixture.

4. Marinate the pork butt for approximately 4 hours and store it in the fridge to keep the pork butt fresh.

5. After 4 hours, take the pork butt out of the fridge and thaw it at room temperature.

6. In the meantime, place the fresh blackberries together with blackberry jam, chipotle pepper, apple cider vinegar, orange zest, black pepper, and salt in a blender. Blend until smooth.

7. Transfer the glaze mixture to a saucepan and bring it to a simmer.

8. Remove the glaze mixture from heat and let it cool.

9. Next, plug the wood pellet smoker then fill the hopper with the wood pellet. Turn the switch on and set the wood pellet smoker for indirect heat.

10. Adjust the temperature to 225°F (107°C) and let the wood pellet smoker reaches the desired temperature.

11. Once it reaches the desired temperature, place the marinated pork butt in the wood pellet smoker and smoke it for 6 hours.

12. Baste the glaze mixture over pork butt and repeat it once every hour.

13. Check the internal temperature of the smoked pork butt and once it reaches 205°F (96°C), remove it from the wood pellet smoker.

14. Quickly wrap the smoked pork butt and let it rest for approximately 30 minutes.

15. Unwrap the smoked pork butt and using a fork shred it.

16. Transfer the shredded smoked pork butt to a serving dish and serve.

17. Enjoy!

Whiskey Marinade Smoked Baby Back Ribs with Maple Glaze

(Cooking Time 5 hours 10 minutes)

Ingredients for 10 servings

- Pork butt (5-lb., 2.3-kg.)

THE MARINADE

- Whiskey - ¼ cup
- Maple syrup - ¼ cup
- Soy sauce - ¼ cup
- Sesame oil - 1 teaspoon
- Ground cinnamon - 1 teaspoon
- Ground nutmeg - ¼ teaspoon
- Grated ginger - 1 tablespoon
- White pepper - 1 teaspoon
- Ground cumin - ½ teaspoon
- Ground coriander - ½ teaspoon

THE GLAZE

- Maple syrup - 1 cup
- Apple cider vinegar - 3 tablespoons
- Lemon juice - 2 tablespoons
- Worcestershire sauce - 2 tablespoons
- Fish sauce - 1 tablespoon
- Tomato paste - 3 tablespoons
- Smoked paprika - 2 teaspoons
- Brown sugar - 3 tablespoons

THE HEAT

- Maple wood pellet

METHOD

1. Pour whiskey, maple syrup, soy sauce, and sesame oil into a container. Stir until incorporated.

2. Season the mixture with cinnamon, nutmeg, ginger, pepper, cumin, and coriander. Mix well.

3. Cut and trim the excess fat from the baby back ribs and put the baby back ribs into the marinade mixture.

4. Rub until the baby back ribs are completely coated with the mixture and marinate them for approximately 4 hours.

5. Store the marinated baby back ribs in the fridge to keep them fresh.

6. In the meantime, pour maple syrup into a saucepan then season it with apple cider vinegar, lemon juice, Worcestershire sauce, fish sauce, tomato paste, smoked paprika, and brown sugar.

7. Stir the glaze mixture and bring it to a simmer.

8. Remove the saucepan from heat and let the glaze cool.

9. After 4 hours, take the marinated baby back ribs from the fridge and thaw it at room temperature.

10. In the meantime, plug the wood pellet smoker then fill the hopper with the wood pellet. Turn the switch on and set the wood pellet smoker for indirect heat.

11. Adjust the temperature to 225°F (107°C) and let the wood pellet smoker reaches the desired temperature.

12. Once it reaches the desired temperature, place the marinated baby back ribs in the wood pellet smoker. Smoke the baby back ribs for 3 hours.

13. After 3 hours, baste half of the glaze over the smoked baby back ribs and wrap them with aluminum foil.

14. Return the wrapped baby back ribs to the wood pellet smoker and continue smoking for another 2 hours.

15. Check the internal temperature of the smoked baby back ribs and once it reaches 190°F (88°C), remove it from the wood pellet smoker.

16. Unwrap the smoked baby back ribs and baste the remaining glaze mixture over the ribs.

17. Serve and enjoy!

Juicy Smoked Pork Shoulder with Chili and Coriander Rub

(Cooking Time 6 hours 10 minutes)

INGREDIENTS FOR 10 SERVINGS

- Pork shoulder (4-lbs., 1.8-kg.)

THE RUB

- Smoked paprika - ½ cup
- Brown sugar - ¼ cup
- Salt - 1 teaspoon
- Garlic powder - 2 tablespoons
- Onion powder - 2 tablespoons
- Black pepper - 1 tablespoon
- Chili powder - 1 tablespoon
- Chipotle chili pepper - 1 tablespoon
- Cayenne pepper - 1 teaspoon
- Cumin - 1 teaspoon
- Dry mustard - 1 tablespoon
- Oregano - 1 tablespoon
- Coriander - 1 teaspoon
- Dried thyme - 1 teaspoon

THE SPRAY

- Apple juice - 1 cup
- Water -1/2 cup
- Cider vinegar - ¼ cup

THE HEAT

- Mix of Apple and Pecan wood pellet

METHOD

1. Mix smoked paprika with brown sugar, garlic powder, onion powder, salt, black pepper, chili powder, chipotle chili pepper, cayenne pepper, cumin, dry mustard, oregano, coriander, and dried thyme. Stir until combined.

2. Score the pork shoulder at several places and rub the spice mixture over the pork shoulder.

3. Next, plug the wood pellet smoker then fill the hopper with the wood pellet. Turn the switch on and set the wood pellet smoker for indirect heat.

4. Adjust the temperature to 225°F (107°C) and let the wood pellet smoker reaches the desired temperature.

5. Once it reaches the desired temperature, place the marinated pork butt in the wood pellet smoker and smoke it for 6 hours.

6. Pour apple juice with water and cider vinegar into a spray bottle.

7. Shake to combine and spray the apple mixture over the pork shoulder during the smoking time.

8. Check the internal temperature of the smoked pork shoulder and once it reaches 205°F (96°C), remove it from the wood pellet smoker.

9. Wrap the smoked pork shoulder with aluminum foil and let it rest for 30 minutes.

10. Unwrap the smoked pork shoulder and using a sharp knife shred it into chunks.

11. Transfer the shredded smoked pork shoulder to a serving dish and serve.

12. Enjoy!

Smoked Pork Loin in Honey Garlic Marinade and Sweet Rub

(Cooking Time 3 hours 10 minutes)

INGREDIENTS FOR 10 SERVINGS

- Pork loin (5-lb., 2.3-kg.)

THE MARINADE

- Honey - ¾ cup
- Dijon mustard - ½ cup
- Soy sauce - 2 tablespoons
- Minced garlic - 1 tablespoon
- Diced rosemary - 1 tablespoon
- Diced thyme - 1 teaspoon
- Salt - 1 teaspoon
- Black pepper - ½ teaspoon

THE RUB

- Paprika - ½ cup
- Brown sugar - ¼ cup
- Chili powder - 3 tablespoons
- Cayenne pepper - 1 teaspoon
- Salt - ½ teaspoon
- Ground cumin - 2 tablespoons
- Black pepper - 1 teaspoon
- Mustard powder - 1 tablespoon
- Garlic powder - 1 tablespoon
- Onion powder - 1 tablespoon

THE HEAT

- Mix of Apple and Cherry wood pellet

METHOD

1. Combine honey with Dijon mustard, soy sauce, minced garlic, diced rosemary, diced thyme, salt, and black pepper. Mix well.

2. Score the pork loin at several places and apple the honey mixture over the loin.

3. Wrap the seasoned pork with plastic wrap and marinate the pork loin for at least 4 hours. Store it in the fridge to keep the pork loin fresh

4. After 4 hours, take the marinated pork loin out of the fridge and thaw it at room temperature.

5. In the meantime, mix paprika with brown sugar, chili powder, cayenne pepper, salt, cumin, black pepper, mustard powder, garlic powder, and onion powder.

6. Rub the pork loin with the spice mixture and set aside.

7. Next, plug the wood pellet smoker then fill the hopper with the wood pellet. Turn the switch on and set the wood pellet smoker for indirect heat.

8. Adjust the temperature to 225°F (107°C) and let the wood pellet smoker reaches the desired temperature.

9. Place the seasoned pork loin in the wood pellet smoker and smoke it for 3 hours.

10. Regularly check the internal temperature of the smoked pork loin and once it reaches 145°F (63°C), remove it from the wood pellet smoker.

11. Cut the smoked pork loin into thick slices and serve.

12. Enjoy!

Cinnamon Chili Smoked Pork Belly BBQ

(Cooking Time 3 hours 10 minutes)

INGREDIENTS FOR 10 SERVINGS

- Pork belly (4-lbs., 1.8-kg.)

THE RUB

- Brown sugar - ¼ cup
- Salt - 1 teaspoon
- Chili powder - 2 teaspoons
- Cayenne pepper - ½ teaspoon
- Garlic powder - 2 tablespoons
- Onion powder - 1 tablespoon
- Paprika - 2 teaspoons
- Black pepper - 1 teaspoon
- Ground cinnamon - ½ teaspoon

THE GLAZE

- White wine vinegar - ¼ cup
- Soy sauce - ¼ cup
- Tomato puree - 2 teaspoons
- Tomato paste - 2 tablespoons
- Tabasco - 1 teaspoon
- Garlic powder - 1 teaspoon
- Ginger powder - ¼ teaspoon
- Brown sugar - 3 tablespoons
- Salt - ¼ teaspoon
- Pepper - ½ teaspoon

The Heat

- Alder wood pellet

Method

1. Mix the rub ingredients in a bowl.

2. Add brown sugar, salt, chili powder, cayenne pepper, garlic powder, onion powder, paprika, black pepper, and cinnamon to the bowl. Stir until combined.

3. Score the pork belly at several places and rub the spice mixture over the belly. Let it rest for approximately 30 minutes.

4. Next, plug the wood pellet smoker then fill the hopper with the wood pellet. Turn the switch on and set the wood pellet smoker for indirect heat.

5. Adjust the temperature to 200°F (93°C) and let the wood pellet smoker reaches the desired temperature.

6. Place the seasoned pork belly in the wood pellet smoker and smoke it for an hour.

7. In the meantime, combine white wine vinegar with soy sauce, tomato pure, tomato paste, Tabasco, garlic powder, ginger powder, brown sugar, salt, and pepper. Mix well.

8. After an hour of smoking, take the pork belly out of the wood pellet smoker and baste the glaze mixture over it.

9. Wrap the pork belly in heavy-duty tinfoil and tightly seal the edges of the foil.

10. Continue smoking the pork belly for another 2 hours or until the internal temperature of the smoked pork belly reaches 150°F (65°C).

11. Remove the smoked pork belly from the wood pellet smoker and let it rest for 15 to 30 minutes.

12. Unwrap the smoked pork belly and cut it into cubes. Serve and enjoy!

SMOKED PORK RIBS WITH SWEET AND SPICY SAUCE

(COOKING TIME 5 HOURS 10 MINUTES)

INGREDIENTS FOR 10 SERVINGS

- Pork ribs (6-lb., 2.7-kg.)

THE RUB

- Brown sugar - ¼ cup
- Paprika - 1 ½ tablespoon
- Chili powder - ¾ teaspoon
- Salt - 1 ½ teaspoon
- Ground cinnamon - ½ teaspoon
- Black pepper - ½ teaspoon
- Cayenne pepper - ½ teaspoon

THE SAUCE

- Olive oil - 3 tablespoons
- Diced onion - ½ cup
- Ground cumin - 1 teaspoon
- Ketchup - 1 cup
- Hot sauce - 2 tablespoons
- Brown sugar - ¼ cup
- Apple cider vinegar - 2 tablespoons
- Salt - a pinch
- Pepper - ¼ teaspoon

THE SPRAY

- Apple juice - 1 cup

THE HEAT

- Apple wood pellet

METHOD

1. Cut and trim the excess fat from the pork ribs.

2. Rub the pork ribs with brown sugar, paprika, chili powder, salt, ground cinnamon, chili powder, and black pepper. Set aside.

3. Next, plug the wood pellet smoker then fill the hopper with the wood pellet. Turn the switch on and set the wood pellet smoker for indirect heat.

4. Adjust the temperature to 225°F (107°C) and let the wood pellet smoker reaches the desired temperature.

5. Place the seasoned pork ribs in the wood pellet smoker and smoke it for 5 hours.

6. In the meantime, pour olive oil into a saucepan and preheat it over medium heat.

7. Stir in diced onion and sauté until wilted and aromatic.

8. Add the remaining sauce ingredients--cumin, ketchup, brown sugar, apple cider vinegar, salt, and pepper.

9. Stir the sauce mixture and bring it to a simmer.

10. Regularly check the internal temperature of the smoked pork ribs and once it reaches 190°F (88°C), remove it from the wood pellet smoker.

11. Transfer the smoked pork ribs to a serving dish and drizzle the sauce over the ribs.

12. Serve and enjoy!

Rosemary Garlic Smoked Pork Roast

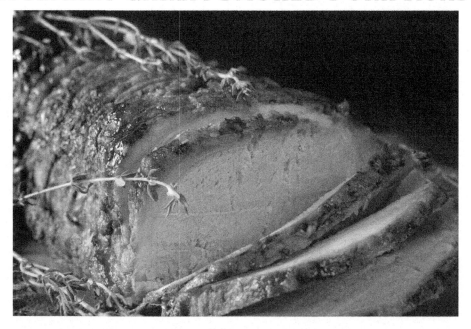

(Cooking Time 6 hours 10 minutes)

Ingredients for 10 servings

- Pork roast (6-lb., 2.7-kg.)

The Rub

- Dried rosemary - 2 tablespoons

- Garlic cloves - 5

- Dried thyme - 1 tablespoon

- Dries sage - 2 teaspoons

- Black pepper - 2 teaspoons

- Onion powder - 1 tablespoon

- Diced red pepper - ½ teaspoon

The Spray

- Apple juice - 1 cup

The Heat

- Apple wood pellet

Method

1. Score the pork roast at several places and set it aside.

2. Next, grate the garlic and place it in a bowl.

3. Add dried rosemary, dried thyme, dried sage, black pepper, onion powder, and red pepper to the grated garlic. Mix well.

4. Rub the garlic and rosemary rub over the pork roast and set aside.

5. After that, plug the wood pellet smoker then fill the hopper with the wood pellet. Turn the switch on and set the wood pellet smoker for indirect heat.

6. Adjust the temperature to 225°F (107°C) and let the wood pellet smoker reaches the desired temperature.

7. Wait until the wood pellet smoker is ready and place the seasoned pork roast in it.

8. Spray apple juice over the pork roast and repeat it once every 30 minutes to an hour.

9. Smoke the pork roast for 6 hours and regularly check the internal temperature.

10. Once it reaches 200°F (93°C), remove the smoked pork roast from the wood pellet smoker.

11. Wrap the smoked pork roast with aluminum foil for 30 minutes and unwrap it.

12. Cut the smoked pork roast into slices and serve. Enjoy!

Chapter-2 Beef

Juicy Smoked Beef Brisket in Coke Marinade

(Cooking Time 8 hours 10 minutes)

INGREDIENTS FOR **10** SERVINGS

- Beef brisket (4-lbs., 1.8-kg.)

THE MARINADE

- Coca-Cola - 4 cups
- Salt - 1 teaspoon
- Black pepper - 1 teaspoon

THE RUB

- Paprika - 1 ½ tablespoon
- Garlic powder - 1 ½ tablespoon
- Onion powder - 1 ½ tablespoon
- Dry mustard - 1 ½ tablespoon
- Salt - 1 teaspoon
- Chili powder - 1 ½ teaspoon
- Black pepper - 1 tablespoon
- Brown sugar - 3 tablespoons

THE SPRAY

- Beer - 2 cups
- Apple cider vinegar - ¼ cup
- Worcestershire sauce - 2 tablespoons

THE HEAT

- Classic blend wood pellet

METHOD

1. Pour Coca-Cola and olive oil into a container then season it with salt and black pepper.

2. Score the beef brisket at several places and put it into the cola mixture.

3. Marinate the beef brisket for at 4 hours and store it in the fridge to keep the beef brisket fresh.

4. After 4 hours, take the beef brisket out of the fridge and thaw it at room temperature.

5. Next, plug the wood pellet smoker then fill the hopper with the wood pellet. Turn the switch on and set the wood pellet smoker for indirect heat.

6. Adjust the temperature to 225°F (107°C) and let the wood pellet smoker reaches the desired temperature.

7. In the meantime, combine paprika, garlic powder, onion powder, dry mustard, salt, chili powder, black pepper, and brown sugar. Mix well.

8. Apply the rub mixture over the beef brisket and set aside.

9. Place the seasoned beef brisket in the wood pellet smoker and smoke it for 8 hours.

10. Pour the beer, apple juice, and Worcestershire sauce into a spray bottle. Shake to combine.

11. Spray the beer mixture over the beef brisket and repeat it once every hour during the smoking time.

12. Regularly check the internal temperature of the smoked beef brisket and once it reaches 205°F (96°C), remove it from the wood pellet smoker.

13. Wrap the smoked beef brisket with a sheet of aluminum foil and let it rest for approximately an hour.

14. After an hour, unwrap the smoked beef brisket and cut it into thin slices.

15. Transfer the smoked beef brisket to a serving dish and enjoy!

SMOKED BEEF BACK RIBS WITH SPICY BLACK TEA RUB

(COOKING TIME 4 HOURS 30 MINUTES)

INGREDIENTS FOR **10** SERVINGS

- Beef back ribs (6-lb., 2.7-kg.)

THE RUB

- Black Tea - 2 tablespoons

- Brown sugar - 3 tablespoons

- Kosher salt - 1 ½ teaspoon

- Paprika - 3 tablespoons

- Chili powder - 1 ½ tablespoon

- Red pepper - ¼ teaspoon

- Garlic powder - 1 ½ tablespoon

- Cumin - 1 teaspoon

- Ground cinnamon - ½ teaspoon

THE HEAT

- Apple wood pellet

METHOD

1. Plug the wood pellet smoker then fill the hopper with the wood pellet. Turn the switch on and set the wood pellet smoker for indirect heat.

2. Adjust the temperature to 250°F (121°C) and let the wood pellet smoker reaches the desired temperature.

3. Next, trim the excess fat of the beef back ribs and move to the seasoning.

4. Grind the black tea into powder and mix with brown sugar, kosher salt, paprika, chili powder, red pepper, garlic powder, cumin, and ground cinnamon.

5. Apply the seasoning mixture over the beef back ribs and set aside.

6. Wait until the wood pellet smoker reaches the desired temperature and place the seasoned beef back ribs in it with the ribs bone side down.

7. Close the lid and smoke the beef back ribs for 3 hours.

8. Check the internal temperature of the smoked beef back ribs and once it reaches 165°F (74°C), remove it from the wood pellet smoker.

9. Place the smoked beef back ribs on a sheet of aluminum foil and wrap it tightly.

10. Return the wrapped beef back ribs to the wood pellet smoker and continue smoking it until the internal temperature reaches 190°F (88°C). It will take approximately an hour or two.

11. Once it is done, take the wrapped beef back ribs out of the wood pellet smoker and let it rest for 30 minutes.

12. Unwrap the smoked beef back ribs and transfer it to a serving dish.

13. Cut the smoked beef back ribs into individual slices and serve.

14. Enjoy!

Sticky Ginger Smoked Beef Short Ribs with Cajun Seasoning

(Cooking Time 6 hours 10 minutes)

INGREDIENTS FOR 10 SERVINGS

- Beef short ribs (5-lb., 2.3-kg.)

The Rub

- Garlic powder - 2 tablespoons
- Onion powder - 2 tablespoons
- Cajun seasoning - 2 tablespoons
- Brown sugar - ¼ cup
- Chili powder - 2 teaspoons
- Kosher salt - ½ teaspoon
- Paprika - 2 teaspoons
- Oregano - 1 tablespoon
- Olive oil - 3 tablespoons

The Glaze

- Soy sauce - 1 cup
- Canola oil - 3 tablespoons
- Rice wine vinegar - 1 tablespoon
- Beef broth - 1 cup
- Brown sugar - ¾ cup
- Garlic powder - 1 tablespoon
- Ginger powder - 1 teaspoon
- Black pepper - ½ teaspoon
- Cayenne pepper - ½ teaspoon

The Heat

- Cherry wood pellet

METHOD

1. Plug the wood pellet smoker then fill the hopper with the wood pellet. Turn the switch on and set the wood pellet smoker for indirect heat.

2. Adjust the temperature to 225°F (107°C) and let the wood pellet smoker reaches the desired temperature.

3. Combine garlic powder with onion powder, Cajun seasoning, brown sugar, chili powder, salt, paprika, and oregano.

4. Pour olive oil into the seasoning mixture and mix until becoming a paste.

5. Rub the beef short ribs with the seasoning mixture and set aside.

6. Wait until the wood pellet smoker reaches the desired temperature and insert the seasoned beef short ribs into it.

7. Smoke the beef short ribs for 2 hours and flip it. Continue smoking for another 2 hours.

8. After 4 hours of smoking, take the smoked beef short ribs out of the wood pellet smoker and place it on a sheet of aluminum foil.

9. Wrap the beef short ribs with the aluminum foil tightly, but let the other side open.

10. Combine the glaze ingredients--soy sauce, canola oil, beef broth, and rice wine vinegar. Stir until combined.

11. Season the glaze mixture with brown sugar, garlic powder, ginger powder, black pepper, and cayenne pepper. Mix well.

12. Pour the glaze mixture into the aluminum foil with smoked beef short ribs and wrap it tightly. You can also use a disposable aluminum pan and cover it with a sheet of aluminum foil.

13. Return the wrapped beef short ribs to the wood pellet smoker and smoke again for 2 hours.

14. Check the internal temperature of the smoked beef short ribs and once it reaches 200°F (93°C), remove it from the wood pellet smoker.

15. Carefully open the aluminum foil and take the smoked beef short ribs. It will be very hot.

16. Place the smoked beef short ribs on a serving dish and pour the remaining liquid over it.

17. Serve and enjoy!

18. Return the wrapped beef back ribs to the wood pellet smoker and continue smoking it until the internal temperature reaches 190°F (88°C). It will take approximately an hour or two.

19. Once it is done, take the wrapped beef back ribs out of the wood pellet smoker and let it rest for 30 minutes.

20. Unwrap the smoked beef back ribs and transfer it to a serving dish.

21. Cut the smoked beef back ribs into individual slices and serve.

22. Enjoy!

SPECIAL ONION AND HERBS SMOKED BEEF PRIME RIB

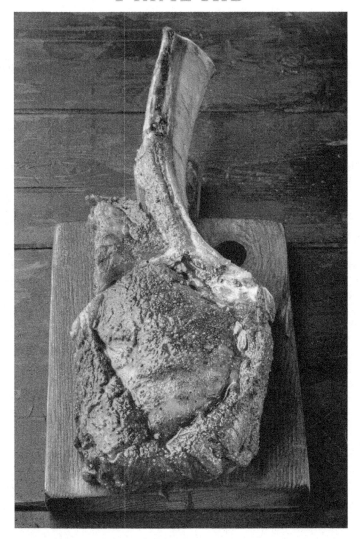

(COOKING TIME 2 HOURS 10 MINUTES)

INGREDIENTS FOR 10 SERVINGS

- Beef chuck roast (5-lb., 2.3-kg.)

THE MARINADE

- Chopped onion - 2 cups
- Minced garlic - 2 tablespoons
- Fresh rosemary - 4 sprigs
- Cumin seeds - 2 tablespoons
- Kosher salt - 1 teaspoon
- Red chili flakes - 2 tablespoons
- Red wine vinegar - 3 tablespoons
- Soy sauce - 1 tablespoon
- Worcestershire sauce - 2 tablespoons
- Lemon juice - 3 tablespoons
- Olive oil - 3 tablespoons
- Beef broth - 1 cup

THE RUB

- Brown sugar - ¼ cup
- Garlic powder - 1 tablespoon
- Onion powder - 1 tablespoon
- Ground rosemary - 1 ½ tablespoon
- Dried thyme - 1 tablespoon
- Smoked paprika - 1 tablespoon
- Kosher salt - 1 teaspoon
- Black pepper - 1 tablespoon
- Dry mustard - 2 teaspoons

THE HEAT

- Hickory wood pellet

METHOD

1. Mix chopped onion with minced garlic, cumin seed, salt, and red chili flakes.

2. Add red wine vinegar, soy sauce, Worcestershire sauce, lemon juice, olive oil, and beef broth. Stir until combined.

3. Chopped the rosemary and rub it over the beef prime rib.

4. Put the beef prime rib into the seasoned liquid and marinate it for 4 hours. Store the marinated beef prime rib in the fridge to keep it fresh.

5. After 4 hours, take the marinated beef prime rib out of the fridge and thaw it at room temperature.

6. Next, plug the wood pellet smoker then fill the hopper with the wood pellet. Turn the switch on and set the wood pellet smoker for indirect heat.

7. Adjust the temperature to 250°F (121°C) and let the wood pellet smoker reaches the desired temperature.

8. In the meantime, combine the rub ingredients--brown sugar, garlic powder, onion powder, ground rosemary, dried thyme, smoked paprika, kosher salt, black pepper, and dry mustard. Mix well.

9. Apply the rub mixture over the marinated beef prime rib and place it in the wood pellet smoker.

10. Smoke the beef prime rib for 2 hours and regularly check the internal temperature of the smoked beef prime rib.

11. Take the smoked beef prime rib out of the wood pellet smoker once the internal temperature reaches 135°F (57°C) for medium. Add more time if you want it to be well done.

12. Place the smoked beef prime rib on a serving dish and cut it into thick slices.

13. Serve and enjoy!

Coffee Rub Smoked Beef Rib eye Tabasco

(Cooking Time 3 hours 10 minutes)

Ingredients for 10 servings

- Beef rib eye (6-lb., 2.7-kg.)

THE RUB

- Ground coffee - 2 tablespoons
- Brown sugar - ¼ cup
- Garlic powder - 2 tablespoons
- Onion powder - 2 tablespoons
- Paprika - 2 tablespoons
- Cumin - 1 tablespoon
- Kosher salt - 1 ½ teaspoon
- Cayenne pepper - ¼ teaspoon
- Chili powder - ½ teaspoon

THE GLAZE

- Beer - 1 cup
- Apple cider vinegar - ¾ cup
- Brewed coffee - 1 cup
- Beef broth - ½ cup
- Vegetable oil - 2 tablespoons
- Worcestershire sauce - 3 tablespoons
- Tabasco - 2 tablespoons
- Kosher salt - ½ teaspoon
- Black pepper - 1 teaspoon

THE HEAT

- Mixed of Oak, Hickory, Apple, and Alder wood pellet

METHOD

1. Mix ground coffee with brown sugar, garlic powder, onion powder, paprika, cumin, kosher salt, chili powder, and cayenne pepper.

2. Rub the seasoning mixture over the beef rib eye and set aside.

3. Next, plug the wood pellet smoker then fill the hopper with the wood pellet. Turn the switch on and set the wood pellet smoker for indirect heat.

4. Adjust the temperature to 250°F (121°C) and let the wood pellet smoker reaches the desired temperature.

5. Place the seasoned beef rib eye in the wood pellet smoker and smoke it for an hour.

6. In the meantime, pour beer, apple cider vinegar, brewed coffee, and beef broth into a disposable aluminum pan.

7. Season the liquid mixture with Worcestershire sauce, Tabasco, salt, and black pepper. Stir until combined.

8. After an hour of smoking, remove the beef rib eye from the wood pellet smoker and transfer it to the aluminum pan with the liquid mixture.

9. Mop the liquid mixture over the beef rib eye and return it to the wood pellet smoker.

10. Continue smoking the beef rib eye for another 2 hours or until the internal temperature of the smoked beef rib eye reaches 135°F (57°C) for medium. Add more time if you want it to be well done.

11. Transfer the smoked beef rib eye to a serving dish and cut it into thick slices.

12. Serve and enjoy!

Cilantro Chili Smoked Beef Tenderloin with Savory Garlic Rub

(Cooking Time 3 hours 10 minutes)

INGREDIENTS FOR 10 SERVINGS

- Beef tenderloin (4-lbs., 1.8-kg.)

THE MARINADE

- Vegetable oil - 1 cup
- White wine vinegar - ½ cup
- Honey - 1 ½ tablespoon
- Lemon juice - 2 teaspoons
- Minced garlic - 2 tablespoons
- Kosher salt - 1 teaspoon
- Dried parsley - 1 teaspoon
- Dried basil - 1 teaspoon
- Dried oregano - ¼ teaspoon
- Black pepper - ½ teaspoon
- Diced cilantro - 2 tablespoons
- Chili powder - 1 tablespoon

THE RUB

- Diced fresh thyme - 1 tablespoon
- Sweet paprika - 3 tablespoons
- Minced garlic - ¼ cup
- Ground red pepper - ½ teaspoon

THE HEAT

- Hickory wood pellet

METHOD

1. Pour vegetable oil, white wine vinegar, honey, and lemon juice into a container.

2. Add minced garlic, kosher salt, dried parsley, dried basil, dried oregano, black pepper, cilantro, and chili powder. Stir until combined.

3. Score the beef tenderloin at several places and put it into the marinade mixture.

4. Marinate the beef tenderloin for at least 4 hours and store it in the fridge to keep the beef tenderloin fresh.

5. After 4 hours, take the marinated beef tenderloin out of the fridge and thaw it at room temperature.

6. Next, plug the wood pellet smoker then fill the hopper with the wood pellet. Turn the switch on and set the wood pellet smoker for indirect heat.

7. Adjust the temperature to 225°F (107°C) and let the wood pellet smoker reaches the desired temperature.

8. In the meantime, combine minced garlic with fresh thyme, sweet paprika, and red pepper. Mix well.

9. Rub the garlic mixture over the marinated beef tenderloin and place it in the wood pellet smoker.

10. Smoke the beef tenderloin for 3 hours or until the internal temperature reaches 140°F (60°C).

11. Once it is done, remove the smoked beef tenderloin from the wood pellet smoker and transfer it to a serving dish.

12. Cut the smoked beef tenderloin into thick slices and serve.

13. Enjoy!

Cayenne Rub Smoked Beef Tri-tip with Brandied Cherry Marinade

(Cooking Time 3 hours 10 minutes)

INGREDIENTS FOR 10 SERVINGS

- Beef tri-tip (4-lbs., 1.8-kg.)

THE MARINADE

- Cherry - 1 cup

- Brandy - ¾ cup

- Diced tarragon leaves - 1 tablespoon

- Black pepper - 1 teaspoon

- Salt - 1 teaspoon

- Soy oil - 3 tablespoons

- Soy sauce - 5 tablespoons

- Balsamic vinegar - 3 tablespoons

- Diced thyme - 2 tablespoons

- Diced rosemary - 1 tablespoon

- Oregano - 1 tablespoon

THE RUB

- Cayenne pepper - 3 tablespoons

- Paprika - ½ cup

- Black pepper - 2 tablespoons

- Garlic powder - 3 tablespoons

- Onion powder - 3 tablespoons

- Salt - ½ teaspoon

- Dried thyme - 1 tablespoon

THE HEAT

- Hickory wood pellet

METHOD

1. Place the cherries in a food processor and process until smooth.

2. Transfer the smooth cherry to a container and pour brandy over it.

3. Season the mixture with tarragon leaves, black pepper, salt, soy oil, soy sauce, balsamic vinegar, thyme, rosemary, and oregano. Mix well.

4. Apply the mixture over the beef tri-tip, and marinate it for approximately 4 hours.

5. Store the marinated beef tri-tip in the fridge to keep it fresh.

6. After 4 hours, take the marinated beef tri-tip out of the fridge and thaw it at room temperature.

7. Mix the rub ingredients--cayenne pepper, paprika, black pepper, garlic powder, onion powder, salt, and thyme. Stir until combined.

8. Rub the marinated beef tri-tip with the spice mixture and set aside.

9. Next, plug the wood pellet smoker then fill the hopper with the wood pellet. Turn the switch on and set the wood pellet smoker for indirect heat.

10. Adjust the temperature to 225°F (107°C) and let the wood pellet smoker reaches the desired temperature.

11. Place the seasoned beef tri-tip in the wood pellet smoker and smoke it for 3 hours.

12. Regularly check the internal temperature and once it reaches 140°F (60°C), remove it from the wood pellet smoker.

13. Place the smoked beef tri-tip on a serving dish and cut it into thick slices.

14. Serve and enjoy!

Chapter-3 Lamb

Lemon Mint Smoked Lamb Leg with Apricot Honey Glaze

(Cooking Time 7 hours 10 minutes)

INGREDIENTS FOR 10 SERVINGS

- Boneless lamb leg (5-lb., 2.3-kg.)

THE MARINADE

- Lemon juice - 1 cup
- Grated lemon zest - 1 tablespoon
- Diced fresh mint leaves - ¼ cup
- Chopped fresh basil - 3 tablespoons
- Oregano - 2 tablespoons
- White vinegar - ¼ cup
- Olive oil - 2 tablespoons
- Minced garlic - 2 tablespoons

THE GLAZE

- Apricot jam - 3 tablespoons
- Honey - 2 tablespoons
- Lemon juice - 1 tablespoon
- Olive oil - 2 tablespoons
- Salt - a pinch
- Black pepper - ½ teaspoon

THE SPRAY

- Apple cider vinegar - 1 cup

THE HEAT

- Cherry wood pellet

METHOD

1. Add the entire marinade mixture--lemon juice, lemon zest, mint leaves, basil, oregano, white vinegar, olive oil, and minced garlic to a container with a lid. Stir until combined.

2. Score the lamb leg at several places and put it into the marinade mixture.

3. Marinate the lamb leg for at least 4 hours and store it in the fridge to keep the lamb leg fresh.

4. After 4 hours, take the marinated lamb leg out of the marinade and thaw it at room temperature.

5. Next, plug the wood pellet smoker then fill the hopper with the wood pellet. Turn the switch on and set the wood pellet smoker for indirect heat.

6. Adjust the temperature to 250°F (121°C) and let the wood pellet smoker reaches the desired temperature.

7. Wait until the wood pellet smoker reaches the desired temperature and place the lamb leg in it.

8. Smoked the lamb leg for 7 hours and spray apple cider vinegar over the lamb leg once every hour.

9. Regularly check the internal temperature of the smoked lamb leg and once it reaches 195°F (91°C), remove it from the wood pellet smoker.

10. Quickly combine the apricot jam with honey, lemon juice, olive oil, salt, and pepper. Stir until incorporated.

11. Baste the glaze mixture over the smoked lamb leg and repeat it until the glaze mixture is completely applied.

12. Once it is done, remove the smoked lamb leg from the wood pellet smoker and transfer it to a serving dish.

13. Serve and enjoy!

Aromatic Mixed Spices Smoked Lamb Shoulder with Black Pepper

(Cooking Time 5 hours 10 minutes)

INGREDIENTS FOR 10 SERVINGS

- Lamb shoulder (5-lb., 2.3-kg.)

THE BRINE

- Cold water - 1 quart
- Kosher salt - 3 tablespoons
- Brown sugar - 3 tablespoons
- Honey - 2 tablespoons
- Minced garlic - 3 tablespoons
- Soy sauce - ¼ cup
- Red chilies - 2 teaspoons
- Fennel seeds- 2
- Star anise - 5
- Cardamom pods - 2
- Lemon grasses - 2
- Ginger powder - 1 teaspoon
- Bay leaves - 2

THE RUB

- Red chili flakes - 1 teaspoon
- Ground cumin - 1 tablespoon
- Smoked paprika -1 tablespoon
- Ground coriander - 2 tablespoons
- Ground turmeric - 1 teaspoon
- Black pepper - 2 teaspoons
- Olive oil - 3 tablespoons

THE SPRAY

- Apple cider vinegar - 1 cup

THE HEAT

- Hickory wood pellet

METHOD

1. Add kosher salt, brown sugar, honey, soy sauce, red chili, fennel seeds, star anise, cardamom pods, lemon grasses, ginger powder, and bay leaves to the cold water. Stir until dissolved.

2. Put the lamb shoulder into the brine mixture and soak it for overnight. Store it in the fridge to keep the lamb shoulder fresh.

3. On the next day, remove the lamb shoulder from the fridge and thaw it at room temperature.

4. Wash and rinse the lamb shoulder. Pat it dry.

5. Next, combine the rub ingredients--red chili flakes, ground cumin, smoked paprika, coriander, turmeric, and black pepper. Mix well.

6. Drizzle olive oil over the rub mixture and stir until becoming a paste.

7. Apply the spice mixture over the lamb shoulder and set it aside.

8. After that, plug the wood pellet smoker then fill the hopper with the wood pellet. Turn the switch on and set the wood pellet smoker for indirect heat.

9. Adjust the temperature to 250°F (121°C) and let the wood pellet smoker reaches the desired temperature.

10. Arrange the lamb shoulder on the grill grate inside the wood pellet smoker and smoke it for 5 hours.

11. Regularly check the internal temperature of the smoked lamb shoulder and once it reaches 195°F (91°C), take it out of the wood pellet smoker.

12. Transfer the smoked lamb shoulder to a serving dish and serve.

13. Enjoy!

COFFEE RUB SMOKED LAMB SHANK WITH COCONUT SUGAR

(COOKING TIME 5 HOURS 10 MINUTES)

INGREDIENTS FOR 10 SERVINGS

- Lamb shank (6-lb., 2.7-kg.)

THE BRINE

- Cold water - 1 quart
- Kosher salt - 3 tablespoons
- Coconut sugar - ¼ cup
- Peppercorns - 2 tablespoons
- Allspice - 1 teaspoon
- Garlic powder - 1 tablespoon
- Dried thyme - 1 teaspoon
- Ground clove - 4
- Bay leaves - 2

THE RUB

- Ground black coffee - ¼ cup
- Kosher salt - 1 ½ teaspoon
- Smoked paprika - 2 tablespoons
- Paprika - 1 tablespoon
- Coconut sugar - ¼ cup
- Ground cumin - 1 tablespoon
- Ground mustard - 1 tablespoon
- Coriander - 1 tablespoon
- Onion powder - 2 tablespoons
- Garlic powder - 2 tablespoons
- Olive oil - ¼ cup

The Spray

- Apple cider vinegar - ½ cup
- Apple juice - ½ cup

The Heat

- A mix of Hickory and Apple wood pellet

Method

1. Pour cold water into a container with a lid.

2. Add kosher salt, coconut sugar, peppercorns, allspice, garlic powder, dried thyme, ground clove, and bay leaves to the brine. Stir until dissolved.

3. Put the lamb shank into the brine mixture and soak it overnight. Store it in the fridge to keep the lamb shank fresh.

4. On the next day, remove the lamb shank from the fridge and take it out of the brine. Thaw it at room temperature.

5. Wash and rinse the lamb shank then pat it dry.

6. Next, mix the rub ingredients--ground black coffee, kosher salt, smoked paprika, paprika, coconut sugar, ground cumin, mustard, coriander, onion powder, and garlic powder.

7. Drizzle olive oil over the spices and mix until becoming a paste.

8. Apply the spice mixture over the lamb shank and set aside.

9. After that, plug the wood pellet smoker then fill the hopper with the wood pellet. Turn the switch on and set the wood pellet smoker for indirect heat.

10. Adjust the temperature to 250°F (121°C) and let the wood pellet smoker reaches the desired temperature.

11. Wait until the wood pellet smoker reaches the desired temperature and place the seasoned lamb shank on the grill grate inside the wood pellet smoker. Smoke the lamb shank for 5 hours.

12. Spray apple juice and apple cider vinegar over the lamb shank and repeat it once every 30 minutes to an hour.

13. Once the internal temperature of the smoked lamb shank reaches 190°F (88°C), take the smoked lamb shank out of the wood pellet smoker and transfer it to a serving dish.

14. Serve and enjoy.

Smoked Lamb Chops with Maple and Peanut Oil Glaze

(Cooking Time 5 hours 10 minutes)

Ingredients for 10 servings

- Lamb chops (4.5-lb., 2.3-kg.)

THE MARINADE

- Buttermilk - 1 cup

- Minced garlic - 2 tablespoons

- Oregano - 1 tablespoon

- Lemon juice - 2 tablespoons

- Kosher salt - 1 teaspoon

- Black pepper - 1 teaspoon

- Ground cumin - 1.2 teaspoon

- Grated lemon zest - 1 teaspoon

THE GLAZE

- Maple syrup - ¼ cup

- Peanut oil - 2 tablespoons

- Soy sauce - 2 tablespoons

- Garlic powder - ½ teaspoon

THE HEAT

- A mix of Apple and Cherry wood pellet

METHOD

1. Season the buttermilk with minced garlic, oregano, lemon juice, kosher salt, black pepper, cumin, and grated lemon zest. Stir until incorporated.

2. Rub the lamb chop with the buttermilk mixture and marinate it for approximately 4 hours. Store it in the fridge to keep the lamb chop fresh.

3. After 4 hours, take the marinated lamb chop out of the fridge and thaw it at room temperature.

4. Next, plug the wood pellet smoker then fill the hopper with the wood pellet. Turn the switch on and set the wood pellet smoker for indirect heat.

5. Adjust the temperature to 250°F (121°C) and let the wood pellet smoker reaches the desired temperature.

6. Arrange the marinated lamb chop on the grill grate inside the wood pellet smoker and smoke it for 5 hours.

7. In the meantime, combine maple syrup with peanut oil, and soy sauce. Stir well.

8. Season the glaze mixture with garlic powder and stir until incorporated.

9. Regularly check the internal temperature of the smoked lamb chop and once it reaches 190°F (88°C), take the smoked lamb chop out of the wood pellet smoker.

10. Quickly baste the glaze mixture over smoked lamb chop and arrange it on a serving dish.

11. Serve and enjoy!

Bourbon Molasses Brine Smoked Lamb Rack with Brown Sugar Glaze

(Cooking Time 3 hours 10 minutes)

INGREDIENTS FOR 10 SERVINGS

- Lamb rack (6-lb., 2.7-kg.)

THE BRINE

- Cold water - 1 quart
- Bourbon - ½ cup
- Kosher salt - ¼ cup
- Molasses - ¼ cup
- Brown sugar - 2 tablespoons
- Worcestershire sauce - 2 tablespoons
- Vanilla extract - 2 teaspoons

THE GLAZE

- Brown sugar - ½ cup
- Unsalted butter - 1 tablespoon
- Chicken broth - ¼ cup
- Soy sauce - 1 tablespoon
- Dijon mustard - 1 tablespoon
- Kosher salt - A pinch
- Ground nutmeg - ¼ teaspoon
- Ground cinnamon - ¼ teaspoon
- Dried thyme - ½ teaspoon
- Dried rosemary - ½ teaspoon
- Rum - 2 tablespoons

THE HEAT

- Apple wood pellet

Method

1. Add bourbon, kosher salt, molasses, brown sugar, Worcestershire sauce, and vanilla extract to the cold water. Stir until dissolved.

2. Put the lamb rack into the brine mixture and soak it overnight. Store it in the fridge to keep the lamb rack fresh.

3. On the next day, remove the lamb rack from the fridge and take it out of the brine. Thaw it at room temperature.

4. Wash and rinse the lamb rack then pat it dry.

5. Next, plug the wood pellet smoker then fill the hopper with the wood pellet. Turn the switch on and set the wood pellet smoker for indirect heat.

6. Adjust the temperature to 250°F (121°C) and let the wood pellet smoker reaches the desired temperature.

7. Wait until the wood pellet smoker reaches the desired temperature and arrange the lamb rack on the grill grate inside the wood pellet smoker. Smoke the lamb rack for an hour.

8. In the meantime, place brown sugar, butter, and chicken broth in a saucepan and bring it to a simmer.

9. Season the glaze mixture with soy sauce, Dijon mustard, kosher salt, ground nutmeg, ground cinnamon, dried thyme, dried rosemary, and rum. Stir well.

10. After an hour of smoking, baste the glaze mixture over the lamb rack and continue smoking for another 2 hours.

11. Once the internal temperature of the smoked lamb rack reaches 140°F (60°C), remove the smoked lamb rack from the wood pellet smoker and transfer it to a serving dish.

12. Baste the remaining glaze mixture over the smoked lamb rack and serve.

13. Enjoy!

CHAPTER-4 CHICKEN

BUTTERMILK BRINE SMOKED WHOLE CHICKEN WITH BROWN SUGAR CHILI RUB

(COOKING TIME 3 HOURS 10 MINUTES)

INGREDIENTS FOR 10 SERVINGS

- Whole Chicken (5-lb., 2.3-kg.)

THE BRINE

- Buttermilk - 3 cups
- Kosher salt - 1 teaspoon
- Pepper - 1 teaspoon
- Oregano - 1 tablespoon

THE RUB

- Brown sugar - ½ cup
- Sweet paprika - ¼ cup
- Chili powder - 2 teaspoons
- Cayenne pepper - 2 teaspoons

THE SPRAY

- Apple cider vinegar - 1 cup

THE HEAT

- Mesquite wood pellet

METHOD

1. Season the buttermilk with salt, pepper, and oregano. Stir until incorporated.

2. Add the chicken to the brine mixture and rub the mixture over the chicken including the chicken cavity.

3. Soak the chicken in the brine mixture for at least 4 hours to overnight and store it in the fridge to keep the chicken fresh.

4. On the next day, take the chicken out of the fridge and thaw it at room temperature.

5. In the meantime, mix brown sugar with sweet paprika, chili powder, and cayenne powder. Stir until combined.

6. Apply the spice mixture over the chicken and set aside.

7. Next, plug the wood pellet smoker then fill the hopper with the wood pellet. Turn the switch on and set the wood pellet smoker for indirect heat.

8. Adjust the temperature to 275°F (135°C) and let the wood pellet smoker reaches the desired temperature.

9. Wait until the wood pellet smoker is ready and insert the seasoned chicken into the wood pellet smoker.

10. Smoke the chicken for 3 hours and spray apple cider vinegar over it once every 20 to 25 minutes.

11. Regularly check the internal temperature of the smoked chicken and once it reaches 165°F (74°C), take the smoked chicken out of the wood pellet smoker.

12. Transfer the smoked chicken to a serving dish and serve.

13. Enjoy!

Turmeric and Rosemary Smoked Chicken Breast

(Cooking Time 2 hours 10 minutes)

Ingredients for 10 servings

- Boneless chicken breast (4-lbs., 1.8-kg.)

THE BRINE

- Cold water - 1 quart
- Kosher salt - 3 tablespoons
- Peppercorns - 1 tablespoon
- Fresh rosemary - 2 sprigs
- Minced garlic - 2 teaspoons
- Fresh lemon - 1

THE RUB

- Brown sugar - 3 tablespoons
- Dried rosemary - 2 tablespoons
- Garlic powder - 1 tablespoon
- Salt - ½ teaspoon
- Pepper - ½ teaspoon
- Oregano - teaspoon
- Turmeric powder - ½ teaspoon

THE GLAZE

- Butter - 2 tablespoons

THE HEAT

- Mix of Hickory and Pecan wood pellet

METHOD

1. Add kosher salt, peppercorns, and minced garlic to the cold water. Stir until dissolved.

2. Cut the lemon into slices and add them to the brine mixture together with rosemary sprigs. Stir well.

3. Score the chicken breast at several places and put the breast into the brine mixture.

4. Soak the chicken breast for approximately 4 hours and store it in the fridge to keep the chicken breast fresh.

5. After 4 hours, remove the chicken from the fridge and take it out of the brine mixture.

6. Wash and rinse the chicken then pat it dry. Set aside.

7. In the meantime, combine brown sugar with dried rosemary, garlic powder, salt, pepper, oregano, and turmeric. Mix well.

8. Rub the chicken breast with the spice mixture and set aside.

9. Next, plug the wood pellet smoker then fill the hopper with the wood pellet. Turn the switch on and set the wood pellet smoker for indirect heat.

10. Adjust the temperature to 275°F (135°C) and let the wood pellet smoker reaches the desired temperature.

11. Arrange the seasoned chicken breast on the grill grate inside the wood pellet smoker and smoke it for 2 hours.

12. Check the internal temperature of the smoked chicken breast and once it reaches 165°F (74°C), remove it from the wood pellet smoker.

13. Take the butter and baste it over the smoked chicken breast.

14. Transfer the smoked chicken breast to a serving dish and serve.

15. Enjoy!

Cinnamon Smoked Chicken Thigh with Whiskey Peach Glaze

(Cooking Time 1 hour 30 minutes)

Ingredients for 10 servings

- Chicken thighs (4-lbs., 1.8-kg.)

The Rub

- Brown sugar - ¼ cup
- Red chili flakes - 1 teaspoon
- Kosher salt - 1 teaspoon
- Allspice - 1 tablespoon
- Ground clove - A pinch
- Ground cinnamon - ¾ teaspoon
- Dried thyme - ½ teaspoon
- Black pepper - ½ teaspoon
- Olive oil - 2 tablespoons

The Glaze

- Chopped peach - 2 cups
- Minced garlic - 2 teaspoons
- Whiskey - ¼ cup
- Brown sugar - 3 tablespoons
- Diced tomatoes - ½ cup
- Smoked paprika - 1 teaspoon
- Worcestershire sauce - 1 teaspoon
- Mustard - 1 teaspoon
- Tomato paste - 1 tablespoon
- Salt - ¼ teaspoon
- Pepper - ½ teaspoon

The Heat

- Mix of Cherry and Alder wood pellet

METHOD

1. Combine brown sugar with red chili flakes, kosher salt, allspice, ground cloves, cinnamon, dried thyme, and black pepper.

2. Drizzle olive oil over the spice and stir it until becoming a paste.

3. Rub the spice mixture over the chicken thigh and set aside.

4. Next, plug the wood pellet smoker then fill the hopper with the wood pellet. Turn the switch on and set the wood pellet smoker for indirect heat.

5. Adjust the temperature to 275°F (135°C) and let the wood pellet smoker reaches the desired temperature.

6. Wait until the wood pellet smoker is ready and arrange the chicken thighs on the grill grate inside the wood pellet smoker.

7. Smoke the chicken thighs for an hour.

8. In the meantime, place the chopped peaches together with minced garlic, whiskey, brown sugar, diced tomatoes, smoked paprika, Worcestershire sauce, mustard, tomato paste, salt, and pepper. Process until smooth.

9. Pour the glaze mixture into a saucepan and bring it to a simmer.

10. Remove the sauce from heat and let it cool.

11. After an hour of smoking, baste half of the glaze mixture over the smoked chicken thigh and wrap it with a sheet of heavy-duty aluminum foil.

12. Return the wrapped chicken thigh to the wood pellet smoker and continue smoking for 30 minutes or until the internal temperature if the smoked chicken reaches 165°F (74°C).

13. Once it is done, take the smoked chicken thigh out of the wood pellet smoker and unwrap it.

14. Transfer the smoked chicken thighs to a serving dish and baste the remaining glaze on top.

15. Serve and enjoy.

CHIPOTLE SMOKED CHICKEN WINGS WITH PINEAPPLE AND COCONUT SUGAR

(COOKING TIME 1 HOUR 15 MINUTES)

INGREDIENTS FOR 10 SERVINGS

- Chicken wings (5-lb., 2.3-kg.)

THE RUB

- Coconut sugar - ¼ cup
- Onion powder - 1 tablespoon
- Paprika - 1 tablespoon
- Chili powder - 1 teaspoon
- Chipotle powder - 1 teaspoon
- Ground cinnamon - 1 teaspoon
- Mustard seeds - 1 teaspoon
- Kosher salt - 1 teaspoon
- Pepper - ½ teaspoon

THE SAUCE

- Olive oil - 2 tablespoons
- Diced onion - ¼ cup
- Minced garlic - 1 teaspoon
- Pineapple juice - 1 cup
- Teriyaki sauce - 3 tablespoons
- Worcestershire sauce - 1 tablespoon
- Lemon juice - 2 tablespoons
- Whisky - 1 tablespoon
- Cayenne pepper - ¼ teaspoon
- Coconut sugar - 2 tablespoons

THE HEAT

- Cherry wood pellet

METHOD

1. Mix the rub ingredients--coconut sugar, onion powder, paprika, chili powder, chipotle powder, ground cinnamon, mustard seeds, kosher salt, and pepper.

2. Rub the chicken wings with the spice mixture and set them aside.

3. Next, plug the wood pellet smoker then fill the hopper with the wood pellet. Turn the switch on and set the wood pellet smoker for indirect heat.

4. Adjust the temperature to 275°F (135°C) and let the wood pellet smoker reaches the desired temperature.

5. Arrange the seasoned chicken wings on the grill grate inside the wood pellet smoker and smoke it for an hour to an hour and 15 minutes.

6. In the meantime, pour olive oil into a saucepan and preheat it over low heat.

7. Stir in diced onion and minced garlic then sauté until wilted and aromatic.

8. Pour pineapple juice together with teriyaki sauce, Worcestershire sauce, lemon juice, and whisky.

9. Season the sauce with cayenne pepper and coconut sugar then stir until incorporated.

10. Bring the sauce to a simmer and remove it from heat.

11. Check the internal temperature of the smoked chicken wings and once it reaches 165°F (74°C), remove the smoked chicken wings from the wood pellet smoker.

12. Take a smoked chicken wing and dip it into the sauce.

13. Repeat with the remaining smoked chicken wings and arrange them on a serving dish.

14. Serve and enjoy.

CHAPTER-5 TURKEY

APPLE AROMA SMOKED WHOLE TURKEY WITH DRY RUB

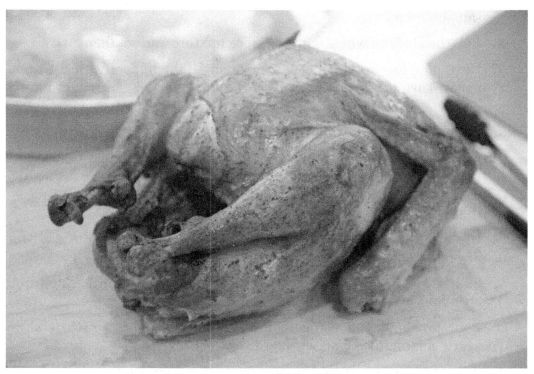

(COOKING TIME 5 HOURS 10 MINUTES)

INGREDIENTS FOR **10** SERVINGS

- Whole turkey (7-lb., 3.2-kg.)

THE BRINE

- Apple juice - 3 quarts

- Orange juice - 1 quart

- Kosher salt - ½ cup

- Brown sugar - ½ cup

- Cloves - 3

- Ground nutmeg - 1 teaspoon

- Ground cinnamon - 1 teaspoon

THE RUB

- Brown sugar - ¼ cup

- Black pepper - 1 teaspoon

- Smoked paprika - 1 tablespoon

- Garlic powder - 1 teaspoon

- Kosher salt - ½ teaspoon

THE HEAT

- Hickory wood pellet

METHOD

1. Pour apple juice and orange juice into a container. Stir a bit.

2. Season the liquid mixture with salt, brown sugar, cloves, nutmeg, and cinnamon. Mix well.

3. Dip the turkey into the brine mixture and soak it for at least 4 hours to overnight. Store it in the fridge to keep the turkey fresh.

4. On the next day, remove the turkey from the fridge and take it out of the brine mixture. Thaw it at room temperature.

5. Wash and rinse the turkey then pat it dray.

6. Next, combine the rub ingredients--brown sugar, black pepper, smoked paprika, garlic powder, and kosher salt. Mix until combined.

7. Rub it over the turkey including the cavity and set it aside.

8. After that, plug the wood pellet smoker then fill the hopper with the wood pellet. Turn the switch on and set the wood pellet smoker for indirect heat.

9. Adjust the temperature to 275°F (135°C) and let the wood pellet smoker reaches the desired temperature.

10. Place the seasoned turkey on the grill grate inside the wood pellet smoker and smoke it for 5 hours.

11. Regularly check the internal temperature of the smoked turkey and once it reaches 165°F (74°C), remove the smoked turkey from the wood pellet smoker.

12. Place the smoked turkey on a serving dish and serve.

13. Enjoy!

Maple Bourbon Smoked Turkey Leg

(Cooking Time 3 hours 10 minutes)

INGREDIENTS FOR **10** SERVINGS

- Turkey legs (4-lbs., 1.8-kg.)

THE MARINADE

- Maple syrup - ½ cup

- Bourbon - ¼ cup

- Apple juice - 2 tablespoon

- Brown sugar - ½ cup

- Kosher salt - 1 teaspoon

- Pepper - ½ teaspoon

THE RUB

- Maple syrup - ½ cup

- Ketchup - ¾ cup

- Red wine vinegar - 3 tablespoons

- Worcestershire sauce - 1 tablespoon

- Ground mustard - 2 teaspoons

- Paprika - 2 teaspoons

- Salt - ¼ teaspoon

- Black pepper - ¼ teaspoon

- Brown sugar - 2 tablespoons

THE HEAT

- Apple wood pellet

METHOD

1. Combine the marinade ingredients--maple syrup, bourbon, apple juice, brown sugar, kosher salt, and pepper. Mix well.

2. Rub the mixture over the turkey legs and set aside.

3. Next, plug the wood pellet smoker then fill the hopper with the wood pellet. Turn the switch on and set the wood pellet smoker for indirect heat.

4. Adjust the temperature to 275°F (135°C) and let the wood pellet smoker reaches the desired temperature.

5. Arrange the turkey legs on the grill grate inside the wood pellet smoker and smoke them for an hour.

6. In the meantime, combine the glaze ingredients--maple syrup, ketchup, red wine vinegar, Worcestershire sauce, ground mustard, paprika, salt, black pepper, and brown sugar. Mix well.

7. After an hour of smoking, baste half the glaze mixture over the turkey legs and continue smoking for another 2 hours. Repeat it once every 30 minutes.

8. Once the internal temperature of the smoked turkey legs reaches 165°F (74°C), remove them from the wood pellet smoker and transfer them to a serving dish.

9. Baste the remaining glaze mixture over the smoked turkey legs and serve.

10. Enjoy!

Mix Herbs Smoked Turkey Wings

(Cooking Time 2 hours 10 minutes)

Ingredients for **10** servings

- Turkey wings (4-lbs., 1.8-kg.)

The Brine

- Cold water - 1 quart

- Lemon juice - 3 tablespoons

- Kosher salt - 3 tablespoons

- Brown sugar - ¼ cup

- Black pepper - ½ teaspoon

- Minced garlic - 2 tablespoons

- Dried rosemary - 1 tablespoon

- Dried thyme - 1 tablespoon

- Dried sage - 1 tablespoon

- Dried marjoram - 1 teaspoons

- Oregano - 1 tablespoon

The Heat

- Alder wood pellet

METHOD

1. Add lemon juice, kosher salt, brown sugar, black pepper, minced garlic, dried rosemary, thyme, sage, marjoram, and oregano to the cold water. Stir until dissolved.

2. Put the turkey wings into the brine mixture and soak them for at least 4 hours or overnight. Store them in the fridge to keep the turkey wings fresh.

3. On the next day, remove the turkey wings from the fridge and take them out of the brine.

4. Wash and rinse the turkey wings then pat them dry.

5. Next, plug the wood pellet smoker then fill the hopper with the wood pellet. Turn the switch on and set the wood pellet smoker for indirect heat.

6. Adjust the temperature to 275°F (135°C) and let the wood pellet smoker reaches the desired temperature.

7. Wait until the wood pellet smoker is ready and arrange the seasoned turkey wings on the grill grate inside the wood pellet smoker and smoke them for 2 hours.

8. Once the internal temperature of the smoked turkey wings reaches 165°F (74°C), remove the smoked turkey wings from the wood pellet smoker.

9. Transfer the smoked turkey wings to a serving dish and serve.

10. Enjoy!

Brandy and Cranberry Glazed Smoked Turkey Breast

(Cooking Time 3 hours 10 minutes)

INGREDIENTS FOR **10** SERVINGS

- Turkey breast (5-lb., 2.3-kg.)

THE MARINADE

- Pineapple chunks - 3 cups

- Soy sauce - ½ cup

- Honey - ½ cup

- Cider vinegar - ½ cup

- Minced garlic - 2 tablespoons

- Grated ginger - ½ teaspoon

- Ground clove - A pinch

THE GLAZE

- Frozen cranberries - 1 cup

- Brandy - ¼ cup

- Granulated sugar - 3 tablespoons

- Ground cinnamon - ½ teaspoon

- Grated lemon zest - 1 teaspoon

- Lemon juice - 2 tablespoons

- Ground clove - A pinch

THE HEAT

- Mix of Apple and Cherry wood pellet

METHOD

1. Place pineapple chunks in a blender then add soy sauce, honey, cider vinegar, minced garlic, grated ginger, and clove. Process until smooth.

2. Score the turkey breast at several places and rub with the pineapple marinade.

3. Marinate the turkey breast for approximately 6 hours and store it in the fridge to keep the turkey breast fresh.

4. After 6 hours, take the marinated turkey breast out of the fridge and thaw it at room temperature.

5. In the meantime, put the frozen cranberries into a blender and pour brandy into it.

6. Add sugar, cinnamon, lemon zest, lemon juice, and clove to the blender. Process until smooth.

7. Transfer the glaze mixture to a saucepan and bring it to a simmer.

8. Remove from heat and let the sauce cool.

9. Next, plug the wood pellet smoker then fill the hopper with the wood pellet. Turn the switch on and set the wood pellet smoker for indirect heat.

10. Adjust the temperature to 275°F (135°C) and let the wood pellet smoker reaches the desired temperature.

11. Place the marinated turkey breast in the wood pellet smoker and smoke it for 3 hours.

12. Baste the glaze mixture over the turkey breast and repeat it once every 30 minutes.

13. Once the internal temperature of the smoked turkey breast reaches 165°F (74°C), remove the smoked turkey breast from the wood pellet smoker.

14. Transfer the smoked turkey breast to a serving dish and serve.

15. Enjoy!

CHAPTER-6 FISH

CORIANDER RUB SMOKED SALMON FILLET

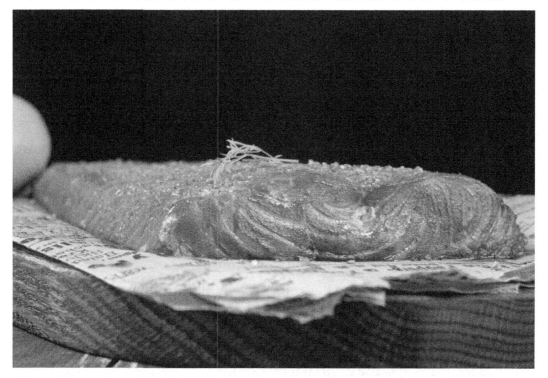

(COOKING TIME 1 HOUR 10 MINUTES)

INGREDIENTS FOR **10** SERVINGS

- Salmon fillet (5-lb., 2.3-kg.)

THE RUB

- Ground coriander - 2 tablespoons

- Black peppercorns - 1 teaspoon

- Brown sugar - ½ cup

- Dill weed - 1 teaspoon

- Celery seeds - ½ teaspoon

- Cumin - 1 teaspoon

- Fennel seeds - ½ teaspoon

- Garlic powder - 1 tablespoon

- Onion powder - ½ tablespoon

- Paprika - 1 teaspoon

- Chili powder - ½ teaspoon

- Kosher salt - 1 teaspoon

- Black pepper - ¼ teaspoon

THE HEAT

- Alder wood pellet

METHOD

1. Place the ground coriander in a bowl together with black peppercorns, brown sugar, dill weed, celery seeds, cumin, fennel seeds, garlic powder, onion powder, paprika, chili powder, salt, and pepper. Mix until combined.

2. Rub the spice mixture over the salmon fillet and set aside.

3. Next, plug the wood pellet smoker then fill the hopper with the wood pellet. Turn the switch on and set the wood pellet smoker for indirect heat.

4. Adjust the temperature to 200°F (93°C) and let the wood pellet smoker reaches the desired temperature.

5. Place the seasoned salmon fillet in the wood pellet smoker and smoke it for approximately 1 hour.

6. Once the internal temperature of the smoked salmon fillet reaches 145°F (63°C), remove it from the wood pellet smoker. The smoked salmon fillet will flake.

7. Place the smoked salmon fillet on a serving dish and serve.

8. Enjoy!

Aromatic Smoked Whole Trout with Lemon and Herbs

(Cooking Time 1 hour 10 minutes)

Ingredients for 10 servings

- Whole trout (6-lb., 2.7-kg.)

The Marinade

- Olive oil - ½ cup

- Lemon juice - 3 tablespoons

- Chopped fresh cilantro - 1 tablespoon

- Chopped fresh basil - 1 teaspoon

- Chopped fresh rosemary - 1 teaspoon

- Chopped fresh thyme - 1 teaspoon

The Heat

- Mesquite wood pellet

Method

1. Mix olive oil with lemon juice then season it with chopped cilantro, basil, rosemary, and thyme. Stir well.

2. Rub the seasoning mixture over the whole trout and marinate it for approximately 30 minutes to an hour.

3. Next, plug the wood pellet smoker then fill the hopper with the wood pellet. Turn the switch on and set the wood pellet smoker for indirect heat.

4. Adjust the temperature to 225°F (107°C) and let the wood pellet smoker reaches the desired temperature.

5. Wait until the wood pellet smoker reaches the desired temperature and place the seasoned trout in the wood pellet smoker.

6. Smoke the trout for approximately an hour or until the internal temperature reaches 145°F (63°C).

7. Once it is done, remove the smoked trout from the wood pellet smoker and transfer it to a serving dish.

8. Serve and enjoy!

LIME AND COCONUT MARINADE SMOKED WHOLE SALMON

(COOKING TIME 1 HOUR 30 MINUTES)

INGREDIENTS FOR 10 SERVINGS

- Whole salmon (6-lb., 2.7-kg.)

THE MARINADE

- Coconut milk - 1 cup

- Fresh limes - 2

- Soy sauce - 2 tablespoons

- Fish sauce - 1 tablespoon

- Chili powder - ½ teaspoon

- Kosher salt - ½ teaspoon

99

The Heat

- Oak wood pellet

Method

1. Cut the limes into halves and squeeze the juice over the coconut milk.

2. Season the liquid mixture with soy sauce, fish sauce, chili powder, and salt. Stir until incorporated.

3. Put the whole salmon into the liquid mixture and make sure that the seasoning mixture completely covers the salmon.

4. Marinate the salmon for an hour and store it in the fridge to keep the salmon fresh.

5. Next, plug the wood pellet smoker then fill the hopper with the wood pellet. Turn the switch on and set the wood pellet smoker for indirect heat.

6. Adjust the temperature to 225°F (107°C) and let the wood pellet smoker reaches the desired temperature.

7. When the wood pellet smoker is ready, place the salmon in the wood pellet smoker and smoke it until flakes. It will take for approximately an hour and 30 minutes.

8. Once it is done, take the smoked salmon out of the wood pellet smoker and place it on a serving dish.

9. Serve and enjoy!

GINGERY SMOKED TILAPIA WITH SESAME OIL

(COOKING TIME 1 HOUR 30 MINUTES)

INGREDIENTS FOR 10 SERVINGS

- Tilapia fillet (5-lb., 2.3-kg.)

THE MARINADE

- Sesame oil - 1 tablespoon
- Soy sauce - ¼ cup
- Rice wine vinegar - 2 tablespoons
- Grated ginger - ¾ teaspoon
- Minced garlic - 1 teaspoon
- Sherry - 2 tablespoons
- Brown sugar - 2 tablespoons
- Kosher salt - ½ teaspoon

THE HEAT

- Oak wood pellet

METHOD

1. Pour sesame oil, soy sauce, and rice vinegar into a container.
2. Season the liquid mixture with ginger, minced garlic, sherry, brown sugar, and kosher salt. Stir until incorporated.
3. Put the tilapia fillet into the seasoning mixture and marinate it for an hour.
4. Next, plug the wood pellet smoker then fill the hopper with the wood pellet. Turn the switch on and set the wood pellet smoker for indirect heat.
5. Adjust the temperature to 225°F (107°C) and let the wood pellet smoker reaches the desired temperature.
6. Place the seasoned tilapia fillet in the wood pellet smoker and smoke it for an hour.
7. Check the internal temperature of the smoked tilapia and once it reaches 145°F (63°C), remove the smoked tilapia from the wood pellet smoker.
8. Place the smoked tilapia on a serving dish and serve. Enjoy!

CHAPTER-7 SEAFOOD

BUTTERY SMOKED LOBSTER TAILS GARLIC

(COOKING TIME 45 MINUTES)

INGREDIENTS FOR 10 SERVINGS

- Lobster tail (4-lbs., 1.8-kg.)

THE SPICES

- Salted butter - ¼ cup
- Garlic powder - 1 teaspoon
- Pepper - ¼ teaspoon

THE HEAT

- Mesquite wood pellet

METHOD

1. Using scissors cut the lobster tails lengthwise along the top and gently pull the shells into halves apart from each other. Set aside.

2. Melt the salted butter over low heat then season it with garlic and pepper. Stir well.

3. Pour the melted butter over the tail meat and set aside.

4. Next, plug the wood pellet smoker then fill the hopper with the wood pellet. Turn the switch on and set the wood pellet smoker for indirect heat.

5. Adjust the temperature to 225°F (107°C) and let the wood pellet smoker reaches the desired temperature.

6. Arrange the lobster tails in the wood pellet smoker and smoke them for 45 minutes.

7. Baste the remaining butter mixture over the lobster tails once every 15 minutes.

8. Once the internal temperature of the smoked lobster tails reaches 140°F (60°C), remove them from the wood pellet smoker.

9. Transfer the smoked lobster tails to a serving dish and serve.

10. Enjoy!

Brown Sugar Lemon Smoked Oyster

(Cooking Time 30 minutes)

INGREDIENTS FOR 10 SERVINGS

- Oyster (3-lb., 1.4-kg.)

THE SPICES

- Dried thyme - 1 teaspoon

- Brown sugar - 3 tablespoons

- Grated lemon zest - 1 teaspoon

- Lemon juice - 3 tablespoons

- Vodka - 2 tablespoons

- Kosher salt - ¼ teaspoon

- Black pepper - ¼ teaspoon

The Heat

- Oak wood pellet

Method

1. Combine dried thyme, brown sugar, lemon zest, lemon juice, vodka, salt, and black pepper. Mix well.

2. Season the oysters with the spice mixture and spread them in a disposable aluminum pan. Set aside.

3. Next, plug the wood pellet smoker then fill the hopper with the wood pellet. Turn the switch on and set the wood pellet smoker for indirect heat.

4. Adjust the temperature to 225°F (107°C) and let the wood pellet smoker reaches the desired temperature.

5. Insert the aluminum pan into the wood pellet smoker and smoke the oyster for 30 minutes.

6. Once it is done, take the smoked oysters out of the wood pellet smoker and transfer them to a serving dish.

7. Serve and enjoy!

GINGER AND MINT SMOKED SCALLOPS

(COOKING TIME 45 MINUTES)

INGREDIENTS FOR 10 SERVINGS

- Scallops (4-lbs., 1.8-kg.)

THE SPICES

- Ginger powder - ½ teaspoon
- Diced mint leaves - 1 teaspoon
- Brown sugar - 3 tablespoons
- Lemon juice - 2 tablespoons
- Olive oil - 3 tablespoons
- Kosher salt - ½ teaspoon
- Tamari - 3 tablespoons
- Black pepper - ½ teaspoon

THE HEAT

- Alder wood pellet

METHOD

1. Mix ginger with chopped mint leaves, brown sugar, salt, and black pepper.

2. Drizzle olive oil, lemon juice, and tamari over the spices. Stir until becoming a paste.

3. Carefully season the scallops with the seasoning mixture and spread them in a disposable aluminum pan.

4. Next, plug the wood pellet smoker then fill the hopper with the wood pellet. Turn the switch on and set the wood pellet smoker for indirect heat.

5. Adjust the temperature to 225°F (107°C) and let the wood pellet smoker reaches the desired temperature.

6. Insert the aluminum pan into the wood pellet smoker and smoke the scallops for 45 minutes.

7. Once the internal temperature of the smoked scallops reaches 145°F (63°C), remove them from the wood pellet smoker.

8. Transfer the smoked o

9. Once it is done, take the smoked oysters out of the wood pellet smoker and transfer them to a serving dish.

10. Serve and enjoy!

Lime Honey Smoked Shrimps with Celery

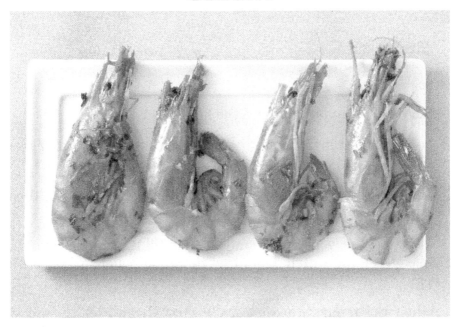

(Cooking Time 20 minutes)

Ingredients for 10 servings

- Fresh shrimps (4-lbs., 1.8-kg.)

The Spices

- Lime juice - 2 tablespoons
- Honey - 1 tablespoon
- Olive oil - 3 tablespoons
- Minced garlic - 2 teaspoons
- Celery seeds - ½ teaspoon
- Kosher salt - ¼ teaspoon
- Black pepper - ¼ teaspoon

109

The Glaze

- Honey - 2 tablespoons

The Heat

- Alder wood pellet

Method

1. Peel the shrimps and discard the heads. Set aside.

2. Mix the liquid ingredients then season it with minced garlic, celery seeds, salt, and black pepper. Stir well.

3. Rub the shrimps with the spice mixture and spread them in a disposable aluminum pan.

4. Next, plug the wood pellet smoker then fill the hopper with the wood pellet. Turn the switch on and set the wood pellet smoker for indirect heat.

5. Adjust the temperature to 225°F (107°C) and let the wood pellet smoker reaches the desired temperature.

6. Insert the aluminum pan with shrimps and smoke them for 20 minutes.

7. Once it is done, remove the smoked shrimps from the wood pellet smoker and transfer them to a serving dish.

8. Drizzle honey over the smoked shrimps and stir a bit.

9. Serve and enjoy.

CHAPTER-8 GAMES

YOGURT MARINADE SMOKED QUAILS WITH PEANUT CHILI SAUCE

(COOKING TIME 2 HOURS 10 MINUTES)

INGREDIENTS FOR 10 SERVINGS

- Quails (3-lb., 1.4-kg.)

THE MARINADE

- Greek yogurt - 1 ½ cup

- Lemon juice - 3 tablespoons

- Grated ginger - 1 teaspoon

- Paprika - 1 tablespoon

- Ground coriander - 1 tablespoon

- Ground cumin - 1 teaspoon

- Ground turmeric - ½ teaspoon

- Chopped cilantro - 3 tablespoons

- Kosher salt - ½ teaspoon

THE SAUCE

- Peanut butter - ¼ cup

- Roasted peanut - ¼ cup

- Chopped cilantro - 2 tablespoons

- Green chili flakes - 1 teaspoon

- Lemon juice - 1 tablespoon

- Soy sauce - 1 teaspoon

- Brown sugar - 1 teaspoon

- Ginger powder - ¼ teaspoon

- Garlic powder - ¼ teaspoon

- Sesame oil - 1 teaspoon

The Heat

- Hickory wood pellet

Method

1. Pour yogurt into a container together with lemon juice.

2. Season the liquid mixture with grated ginger, paprika, coriander, cumin, turmeric, cilantro, and salt. Mix well.

3. Rub the quails with the yogurt mixture and marinate them for at least 4 hours. Store them in the fridge to keep the quails fresh.

4. After 4 hours, take the quails out of the fridge and thaw them at room temperature.

5. Next, plug the wood pellet smoker then fill the hopper with the wood pellet. Turn the switch on and set the wood pellet smoker for indirect heat.

6. Adjust the temperature to 250°F (121°C) and let the wood pellet smoker reaches the desired temperature.

7. Arrange the marinated quails on the grill grate inside the wood pellet smoker and smoke them for 2 hours.

8. In the meantime, place the entire sauce ingredients--peanut butter, roasted peanuts, chopped cilantro, chili flakes, lemon juice, soy sauce, brown sugar, ginger powder, garlic powder, and sesame oil in a food processor. Process until smooth.

9. Check the internal temperature of the smoked quails and once it reaches 165°F (74°C), remove the smoked quails from the wood pellet smoker.

10. Transfer the smoked quails to a serving dish and serve.

11. Enjoy!

Beer Marinade Smoked Pheasant with Lemon Honey Glaze

(Cooking Time 2 hours 10 minutes)

INGREDIENTS FOR **10** SERVINGS

- Pheasant (4-lbs., 1.8-kg.)

THE MARINADE

- Beer - 1 ½ cup

- Butter - ¼ cup

- Minced garlic - 2 teaspoons

- Kosher salt - ¼ teaspoon

- Black pepper - 1 teaspoon

THE GLAZE

- Honey - ¾ cup

- Lemon juice - ¼ cup

- Pepper - ¼ teaspoon

- Dried thyme - 1 teaspoon

THE HEAT

- Cherry wood pellet

METHOD

1. Melt butter and combine with beer.

2. Season the liquid mixture with minced garlic, salt, and pepper. Stir until incorporated.

3. Rub the beer mixture over the pheasant and marinate it for at least 4 hours. Store it in the fridge to keep the pheasant fresh.

4. After 4 hours, take the marinated pheasant out of the fridge and thaw it at room temperature.

5. Next, plug the wood pellet smoker then fill the hopper with the wood pellet. Turn the switch on and set the wood pellet smoker for indirect heat.

6. Adjust the temperature to 250°F (121°C) and let the wood pellet smoker reaches the desired temperature.

7. Place the marinated pheasant on the grill grate inside the wood pellet smoker and smoke it for an hour.

8. In the meantime, combine honey with lemon juice, pepper, and dried thyme. Stir well.

9. After an hour of smoking, baste the glaze mixture over the pheasant and repeat it once every 20 minutes.

10. Continue smoking the pheasant for another hour and regularly check the internal temperature.

11. Once it reaches 165°F (74°C), remove the smoked pheasant from the wood pellet smoker.

12. Quickly wrap the smoked pheasant with aluminum foil and let it rest for approximately 30 minutes.

13. Unwrap the smoked pheasant and place it on a serving dish.

14. Serve and enjoy!

CELERY AND APPLE STUFFED SMOKED CORNISH HEN WITH CINNAMON RUB

(COOKING TIME 2 HOURS 10 MINUTES)

INGREDIENTS FOR 10 SERVINGS

- Cornish hens (6-lb., 2.7-kg.)

THE RUB

- Brown sugar - ¾ cup
- Smoked paprika - ½ cup
- Kosher salt - 1 ½ teaspoon
- Chili powder - 1 tablespoon
- Garlic powder - 1 tablespoon
- Onion powder - 2 teaspoons
- Black pepper - ½ teaspoon
- Ground cinnamon - ½ teaspoon
- Cayenne pepper - 1 teaspoon

THE STUFF

- Fresh lemons - 2
- Fresh apples - 2
- Chopped leek - 2 tablespoons
- Chopped celery stalks - 2 tablespoons

THE HEAT

- Cherry wood pellet

METHOD

1. Combine the rub ingredients--brown sugar, smoked paprika, kosher salt, chili powder, garlic powder, onion powder, black pepper, cinnamon, and cayenne pepper. Mix well.

2. Rub the spice mixture over the Cornish hens, including the cavity, and set aside.

3. Next, cut lemon and apples into slices.

4. Combine the sliced lemon and apple with chopped leek and celery stalks. Mix well.

5. Fill the cavity with the stuff mixture and set aside.

6. After that, plug the wood pellet smoker then fill the hopper with the wood pellet. Turn the switch on and set the wood pellet smoker for indirect heat.

7. Adjust the temperature to 250°F (121°C) and let the wood pellet smoker reaches the desired temperature.

8. Place the stuffed Cornish hens on the grill grate inside the wood pellet smoker and smoke them for 2 hours.

9. Once the internal temperature of the smoked Cornish hens reaches 165°F (74°C), remove them from the wood pellet smoker.

10. Transfer the smoked Cornish hens to a serving dish and serve.

11. Enjoy!

MAPLE ORANGE SMOKED WILD DUCK

(COOKING TIME 2 HOURS 10 MINUTES)

INGREDIENTS FOR **10** SERVINGS

- Wild ducks (6-lb., 2.7-kg.)

THE BRINE

- Cold water - 2 quarts

- Kosher salt - ¼ cup

- Brown sugar - ½ cup

- Lemon juice - ¼ cup

THE GLAZE

- Maple syrup - ¼ cup

- Orange juice - 1 cup

- Honey - ¼ cup

- Balsamic vinegar - ¼ cup

- Dijon mustard - 1 tablespoon

- Dried thyme - ½ teaspoon

- Garlic powder - 1 teaspoon

THE HEAT

- Mix of Apple and Cherry wood pellet

METHOD

1. Add brown sugar, salt, and lemon juice to the cold water. Stir until dissolved.

2. Put the ducks into the brine mixture and soak them overnight. Store them in the fridge to keep the duck fresh.

3. On the next day, remove the ducks from the fridge and thaw them at room temperature.

4. Wash and rinse the duck the pat them dry. Set aside.

5. Next, combine the glaze mixture--maple syrup, orange juice, honey, balsamic vinegar, Dijon mustard, thyme, and garlic powder. Stir until incorporated and set aside.

6. After that, plug the wood pellet smoker then fill the hopper with the wood pellet. Turn the switch on and set the wood pellet smoker for indirect heat.

7. Adjust the temperature to 275°F (135°C) and let the wood pellet smoker reaches the desired temperature.

8. Place the ducks on the grill grate inside the wood pellet smoker and smoke them for 2 hours.

9. Baste the glaze mixture over the ducks and repeat it once every 30 minutes.

10. Once the internal temperature of the smoked ducks reaches 165°F (74°C), remove the smoked ducks from the wood pellet smoker.

11. Serve and enjoy!

CHAPTER-9 VEGETABLES

LEMON HERBS SMOKED ASPARAGUS

(COOKING TIME 1 HOUR)

INGREDIENTS FOR **10** SERVINGS

- Asparagus (2-lbs., 0.9-kg.)

THE RUB

- Minced garlic - 2 tablespoons

- Grated lemon zest - 1 teaspoon

- Diced parsley - 1 teaspoon

- Diced fresh chives - 1 teaspoon

- Diced fresh rosemary - 1 teaspoon

- Salt - ¼ teaspoon

- Black pepper - ¼ teaspoon

- Olive oil - 2 tablespoons

- Lemon juice - 2 tablespoons

THE HEAT

- Apple wood pellet

METHOD

1. Cut and trim the asparagus. Set aside.

2. Mix minced garlic with lemon zest, parsley, chives, rosemary, salt, and black pepper.

3. Drizzle olive oil and lemon juice over the spice mixture. Stir until becoming a paste.

4. Rub the asparagus with the seasoning paste and spread the asparagus in a disposable aluminum pan.

5. Next, plug the wood pellet smoker then fill the hopper with the wood pellet. Turn the switch on and set the wood pellet smoker for indirect heat.

6. Adjust the temperature to 225°F (107°C) and let the wood pellet smoker reaches the desired temperature.

7. Insert the aluminum pan with asparagus into the wood pellet smoker and smoke it for an hour or until tender.

8. Once it is done, remove the smoked asparagus from the wood pellet smoker and transfer it to a serving dish.

9. Serve and enjoy!

BROWN SUGAR SMOKED ONION WITH CHILI AND CAYENNE

(COOKING TIME 1 HOUR 30 MINUTES)

Ingredients for 10 servings

- Onions (2-lbs., 0.9-kg.)

The Rub

- Brown sugar - ¼ cup
- Paprika - 3 tablespoons
- Salt - ¼ teaspoon
- Pepper - ¼ teaspoon
- Chili powder - 1 teaspoon
- Cayenne pepper - ½ teaspoon
- Onion powder - 1 teaspoon
- Mustard powder - ½ teaspoon
- Ground cinnamon - 1 teaspoon

The Glaze

- Butter - 2 tablespoons

The Heat

- Cherry wood pellet

METHOD

1. Peel and cut the onions into halves. Set aside.

2. Mix brown sugar with paprika, salt, pepper, chili powder, cayenne pepper, onion powder, mustard powder, and ground cinnamon. Stir until incorporated.

3. Rub the onion with the seasoning mixture and arrange the onion on a disposable aluminum pan.

4. Next, plug the wood pellet smoker then fill the hopper with the wood pellet. Turn the switch on and set the wood pellet smoker for indirect heat.

5. Adjust the temperature to 225°F (107°C) and let the wood pellet smoker reaches the desired temperature.

6. Insert the aluminum pan with onion into the wood pellet smoker and smoke it for an hour.

7. After an hour of smoking, baste butter over the onions and continue smoking for about 30 minutes.

8. Once it is done, take the smoked onions out of the wood pellet smoker and serve.

9. Enjoy!

SMOKED CABBAGE GARLIC WITH CANOLA OIL

(COOKING TIME 3 HOURS)

INGREDIENTS FOR **10** SERVINGS

- Whole cabbages (3-lb., 1.4-kg.)

THE SPICES

- Butter - ¼ cup
- Canola oil - 2 tablespoons
- Garlic powder - 1 teaspoon
- Ground ginger - ½ teaspoon
- Salt - ¼ teaspoon
- Chili powder - ¼ teaspoon
- Ground turmeric - ¼ teaspoon

THE HEAT

- Maple wood pellet

METHOD

1. Melt butter and mix with canola oil.

2. Add garlic powder, ginger, salt, chili powder, and ground turmeric. Mix well.

3. Cut the cabbages into thick slices and baste the mixture over them.

4. Next, plug the wood pellet smoker then fill the hopper with the wood pellet. Turn the switch on and

5. set the wood pellet smoker for indirect heat.

6. Adjust the temperature to 275°F (135°C) and let the wood pellet smoker reaches the desired temperature.

7. Arrange the seasoned cabbage wedges in the wood pellet smoker and smoke them for 3 hours or until tender.

8. Once it is done, take the smoked cabbages out of the wood pellet smoker and transfer them to a serving dish.

9. Serve and enjoy.

SMOKED CAULIFLOWER CURRY WITH CHILI

(COOKING TIME 2 HOURS)

INGREDIENTS FOR **10** SERVINGS

- Whole cabbages (3-lb., 1.4-kg.)

THE SPICES

- Vegetable oil - 2 tablespoons

- Greek yogurt - 1 cup

- Lemon juice - 2 tablespoons

- Grated lemon zest - 1 teaspoon

- Chili powder - ½ teaspoon

- Ground cumin - 1 teaspoon

- Garlic powder - 1 tablespoon

- Curry powder - 1 tablespoon

- Kosher salt - ½ teaspoon

- Black pepper - ½ teaspoon

THE HEAT

- Apple wood pellet

METHOD

1. Combine Greek yogurt with vegetable oil with lemon juice.

2. Season the liquid mixture with grated lemon zest, chili powder, cumin, garlic powder, curry powder, salt, and black pepper. Stir until incorporated.

3. Rub the seasoning mixture over the cabbage and wrap it with aluminum foil.

4. Next, plug the wood pellet smoker then fill the hopper with the wood pellet. Turn the switch on and set the wood pellet smoker for indirect heat.

5. Adjust the temperature to 275°F (135°C) and let the wood pellet smoker reaches the desired temperature.

6. Place the wrapped cauliflower in the wood pellet smoker and smoke it for 2 hours.

7. Once it is done, remove the smoked cauliflower from the wood pellet smoker and let it rest for 15 minutes.

8. Unwrap the smoked cauliflower and serve.

9. Enjoy!

Chapter-10 Sauces
Savory Smoked Hot Chili Sauce

(Cooking Time 1 Hour 10 Minutes)

INGREDIENTS FOR **10** SERVINGS

- Red Chili Peppers (1-lb., 0.5-kg.)

THE SPICES

- Salt - 1 teaspoon

- Olive oil - ¼ cup

- Apple cider vinegar - ½ cup

- Sugar - a pinch

THE HEAT

- Apple wood pellet

METHOD

1. Plug the wood pellet smoker then fill the hopper with the wood pellet. Turn the switch on and set the wood pellet smoker for indirect heat.

2. Adjust the temperature to 225°F (107°C) and let the wood pellet smoker reaches the desired temperature.

3. Remove the top of the chilies and slice the chilies lengthwise. Discard the seeds from the chilies.

4. Take a smaller grill grate and arrange the chilies on it.

5. Place the chilies in the wood pellet smoker and smoke it for 45 minutes to an hour.

6. Once it is done, remove the smoked chilies from the wood pellet smoker and transfer them to a blender.

7. Add olive oil and apple cider vinegar to the blender.

8. Season the chilies with salt and sugar. Process until smooth.

9. Transfer the sauce to a jar and serve.

Smoked Tomato Sauce with Basil

(Cooking Time 2 Hours 10 minutes)

INGREDIENTS FOR **10** SERVINGS

- Large red tomatoes (2-lbs., 0.9-kg.)

THE SPICES

- Olive oil - 3 tablespoons
- Kosher salt - ¼ teaspoon
- Pepper - ½ teaspoon

THE ADDITIONAL INGREDIENTS

- Olive oil - 1 tablespoon
- Diced onion - 1 cup
- Minced garlic - 1 teaspoon
- Salt - A pinch
- Pepper - ½ teaspoon
- Red chili flakes - 2 teaspoons
- Sugar - A pinch
- Dried basil - ½ teaspoon

THE HEAT

- Apple wood pellet

METHOD

1. Cut the tomatoes into halves and baste olive oil on it.

2. Sprinkle salt and pepper over the halved tomatoes. Set aside.

3. Plug the wood pellet smoker then fill the hopper with the wood pellet. Turn the switch on and set the wood pellet smoker for indirect heat.

4. Adjust the temperature to 250°F (121°C) and let the wood pellet smoker reaches the desired temperature.

5. Arrange the tomatoes in the wood pellet smoker and smoke them for 2 hours.

6. Once the smoked tomatoes are done, take them out of the wood pellet smoker and transfer them to a plate.

7. Peel the skin of the smoked tomatoes and set aside.

8. Next, make the sauce.

9. Preheat a saucepan over low heat and pour olive oil into it.

10. Stir in the diced onion and minced garlic then sauté until wilted and aromatic.

11. Add the smoked tomatoes to the saucepan then season with salt, pepper, red chili flakes, sugar, and dried basil.

12. Stir well and bring it to a simmer.

13. Remove the sauce from heat and let it cool.

14. Using an immersion blender, blend the sauce until smooth.

15. Transfer the sauce to a jar and serve.

SMOKED JALAPENO CUMIN SAUCE

(COOKING TIME 1 HOUR 10 MINUTES)

INGREDIENTS FOR 10 SERVINGS

- Green Jalapeno Peppers (1-lb., 0.5-kg.)

THE ADDITIONAL INGREDIENTS

- Chopped onion - 1 cup

- Minced garlic - 1 tablespoon

- Ground cumin - 1 teaspoon

- Oregano - 1 tablespoon

- Salt - ¼ teaspoon

- Chopped green tomatoes - ¼ cup

- Molasses - 2 tablespoons

- Apple cider vinegar - 3 tablespoons

THE HEAT

- Maple wood pellet

METHOD

1. Plug the wood pellet smoker then fill the hopper with the wood pellet. Turn the switch on and set the wood pellet smoker for indirect heat.

2. Adjust the temperature to 225°F (107°C) and let the wood pellet smoker reaches the desired temperature.

3. Cut the jalapeno peppers lengthwise and discard the seeds.

4. Spread the jalapeno peppers in a disposable aluminum pan and smoke them for 45 minutes to an hour.

5. Once it is done, remove the smoked jalapeno peppers from the wood pellet smoker and transfer them to a food processor.

6. Add chopped onion, minced garlic, ground cumin, oregano, salt, tomatoes, molasses, and apple cider vinegar. Process until smooth.

7. Transfer the sauce to a jar and serve.

SMOKED CARROT SAUCE WITH MAPLE AND THYME

(COOKING TIME 1 HOUR 40 MINUTES)

INGREDIENTS FOR 10 SERVINGS

- Baby Carrots (2-lbs., 0.9-kg.)

THE SPICES

- Olive oil - 2 tablespoons

- Salt - ¼ teaspoon

- Black pepper - ¼ teaspoon

- Maple syrup - 2 tablespoons

- Thyme - ½ teaspoon

THE ADDITIONAL INGREDIENTS

- Chopped onion - ¼ cup

- Minced garlic - 2 teaspoons

- Balsamic vinegar - 2 tablespoons

- Tomato paste - 2 tablespoons

- Salt - A pinch

- Pepper - ¼ teaspoon

THE HEAT

- Maple wood pellet

METHOD

1. Plug the wood pellet smoker then fill the hopper with the wood pellet. Turn the switch on and set the wood pellet smoker for indirect heat.

2. Adjust the temperature to 225°F (107°C) and let the wood pellet smoker reaches the desired temperature.

3. Peel the carrots and rub them with olive oil, salt, black pepper, maple syrup, and thyme.

4. Spread the seasoned carrots in a disposable aluminum pan and insert it into the wood pellet smoker.

5. Smoke the carrots for an hour and a half or until tender then remove from the wood pellet smoker.

6. Transfer the smoked carrots to a food processor then add chopped onion, minced garlic, balsamic vinegar, tomato paste, salt, and pepper. Process until smooth.

7. Transfer the smoked carrot sauce to a bowl and serve.

CHAPTER-11 SMOKING MEAT

WOOD PELLET USING TIPS

Before starting to use your Wood Pellet for the first time, and before getting started with some of the most sumptuous recipes you can ever stumble into, here are some of the most important things you need to know about Wood Pellets at first. Indeed, Wood pellets are basically a form of compressed wood and of sawdust that is basically created through the process of exposing certain agents to a certain degree of heat. And one of the most well-known uses of wood pellets is to use it in order to fuel certain cooking smokers and grills. Wood Pellet Smokers and Grills are indeed, known for bringing a very special smoked flavour of wood to the food ingredients you are smoking or to any type of meat. And the smoking taste that you can get from wood pellet smokers is very special and unique that you can never forget the taste of food once you try smoke cooking it with the Wood Pellet Smoker or Grill. And before starting your wood pellet journey, here are some tips of using Wood Pellet Smoker or Grills, in addition to some benefits of Wood Pellet cooking:

1. Wood pellets are mainly characterized by being eco-friendly; basically because most of the Wood Pellets are made of renewable elements and materials. The production of Wood Pellets encourages on the process of repurposing the materials that can be thrown away by people.

2. Wood pellets are usually available in various forms and types; each of which can offer a different flavour. And this includes cherry, alder, apple, maple, oak, mesquite and hickory wood pellets

3. Wood pellets are known for being a lot more efficient in comparison to other types of gas and fossil because wood pellets are mainly able to use about 90% of the contained energy. And then the wood pellets can turn the energy into heat.

4. Wood pellets can help you cook some very delicious dishes with the smoky flavour it can offer you. Thanks to Wood Pellet Smoking method, you will be able to enjoy tastes that are similar to that obtained when using charcoal.

5. Wood pellets can help you produce a very nice flavour and you will be able to easily clean you Wood Pellet Smoker or Grill because there won't be so much ash.

6. Whenever you want to use your wood pellet smoker grill, switch on the charcoal grill by firing up a quantity of charcoal. Then wait for the charcoal to heat up before sprinkling an amount of wood pellets under the rock grate.

7. Within a short period of time, your wood pellets will start igniting. And once you see the pellets sparkle it is a signal that you should start cooking and you will see the nice wood smoke. Close the lid of your wood pellet smoker in order to keep the smoke in.

8. While it's okay to use wood pellets on their own, you'll notice that they burn too quickly without the charcoal. And some people choose to use a smoker box or add foil in order to slow down the process of burning. Usually 2/3 cup of wood pellets can give you about ½ hour of smoke.

9. You can use a pellet tube smoker in order to keep wood pellets in as you combine it with the charcoal. And this can help increase the smokiness of the flavour. Pellet tube smokers are usually affordable and are worth to check it out.

DIFFERENCE BETWEEN BARBECUING AND SMOKING MEAT

You might not believe it, but there are still people who think that the process of Barbequing and Smoking are the same! So, this is something which you should know about before diving in deeper.

So, whenever you are going to use a traditional BBQ grill, you always put your meat directly on top of the heat source for a brief amount of time which eventually cooks up the meal. Smoking, on the other hand, will require you to combine the heat from your grill as well as the smoke to infuse a delicious smoky texture and flavor to your meat. Smoking usually takes much longer than traditional barbecuing. In most cases, it takes a minimum of 2 hours and a temperature of 100 -120 degrees for the smoke to be properly infused into the meat. Keep in mind that the time and temperature will obviously depend on the type of meat that you are using, and that is why it is suggested that you keep a meat thermometer handy to ensure that your meat is doing fine. Keep in mind that this method of barbecuing is also known as "Low and slow" smoking as well. With that cleared up, you should be aware that there are actually two different ways through which smoking is done.

DIFFERENCE BETWEEN COLD AND HOT SMOKING

Depending on the type of grill that you are using, you might be able to get the option to go for a Hot Smoking Method or a Cold Smoking One. The primary fact about these three different cooking techniques which you should keep in mind are as follows:

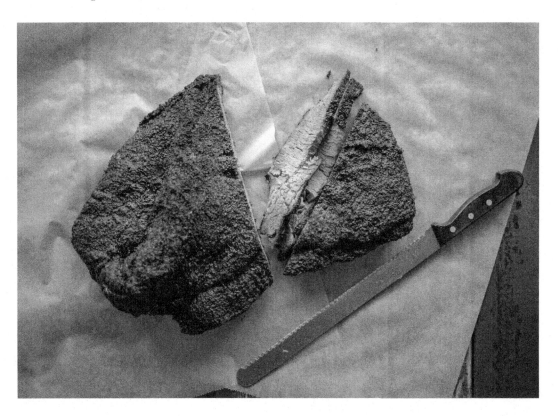

- **HOT SMOKING:** In this technique, the food will use both the heat on your grill and the smoke to prepare your food. This method is most suitable for items such as chicken, lamb, brisket etc.
- **COLD SMOKING:** In this method, you are going to smoke your meat at a very low temperature such as 30 degrees Celsius, making sure that it doesn't come into the direct contact with the heat. This is mostly used as a means to preserve meat and extend their life on the shelf.
- **ROASTING SMOKE:** This is also known as Smoke Baking. This process is essentially a combined form of both roasting and baking and can be performed in any type of smoker with a capacity of reaching temperatures above 82 degrees Celsius.

DIFFERENT SMOKER TYPES

Essentially, what you should know is that right now in the market, you are going to get three different types of Smokers.

Charcoal Smoker

These types of smokers are hands down the best one for infusing the perfect Smoky flavor to your meat. But be warned, though, that these smokers are a little bit difficult to master as the method of regulating temperature is a little bit difficult when compared to normal Gas or Electric smokers.

Electric Smoker

After the charcoal smoker, next comes perhaps the simpler option, Electric Smokers. These are easy to use and plug and play type. All you need to do is just plug in, set the temperature and go about your daily life. The smoker will do the rest. However, keep in mind that the finishing smoky flavor won't be as intense as the Charcoal one.

Gas Smokers

Finally, comes the Gas Smokers. These have a fairly easy mechanism for temperature control and are powered usually by LP Gas. The drawback of these Smokers is that you are going to have to keep checking up on your Smoker every now and then to ensure that it has not run out of Gas.

Different Smoker Styles

The different styles of Smokers are essentially divided into the following.

Vertical (Bullet Style Using Charcoal)

These are usually low-cost solutions and are perfect for first-time smokers.

Vertical (Cabinet Style)

These Smokers come with a square shaped design with cabinets and drawers/trays for easy accessibility. These cookers also come with a water tray and a designated wood chips box as well.

Offset

These type of smokers have dedicated fireboxes that are attached to the side of the main grill. The smoke and heat required for these are generated from the firebox itself which is then passed through the main chamber and out through a nicely placed chimney.

KAMADO JOE

And finally, we have the Kamado Joe which is ceramic smokers are largely regarded as being the "Jack Of All Trades".

These smokers can be used as low and slow smokers, grills, hi or low-temperature ovens and so on.

They have a very thick ceramic wall which allows it to hold heat better than any other type of smoker out there, requiring only a little amount of charcoal.

These are easy to use with better insulation and are more efficient when it comes to fuel control.

The Different Types Of Wood	Suitable For
Hickory	Wild game, chicken, pork, cheeses, beef
Pecan	Chicken, pork, lamb, cheeses, fish.
Mesquite	Beef and vegetables
Alder	Swordfish, Salmon, Sturgeon and other types of fishes. Works well with pork and chicken too.
Oak	Beef or briskets
Maple	Vegetable, ham or poultry
Cherry	Game birds, poultry or pork
Apple	Game birds, poultry, beef
Peach	Game birds, poultry or pork
Grape Vines	Beef, chicken or turkey
Wine Barrel Chips	Turkey, beef, chicken or cheeses
Seaweed	Lobster, mussels, crab, shrimp etc.
Herbs or Spices such as rosemary, bay leaves, mint, lemon peels, whole nutmeg etc.	Good for cheeses or vegetables and a small collection of light meats such as fillets or fish steaks.

DIFFERENT TYPES OF CHARCOAL

In General, there are essentially three different types of Charcoals. All of them are basically porous residues of black color that are made of carbon and ashes. However, the following are a little bit distinguishable due to their specific features.

- **BBQ BRIQUETTES:** These are the ones that are made from a fine blend of charcoal and char.
- **CHARCOAL BRIQUETTES:** These are created by compressing charcoal and are made from sawdust or wood products.
- **LUMP CHARCOAL:** These are made directly from hardwood and are the most premium quality charcoals available. They are completely natural and are free from any form of the additive.

THE BASIC PREPARATIONS

- Always be prepared to spend the whole day and take as much time as possible to smoke your meat for maximum effect.
- Make sure to obtain the perfect Ribs/Meat for the meal which you are trying to smoke. Do a little bit of research if you need.
- I have already added a list of woods in this book, consult to that list and choose the perfect wood for your meal.
- Make sure to prepare the marinade for each of the meals properly. A great deal of the flavor comes from the rubbing.
- Keep a meat thermometer handy to get the internal temperature when needed.
- Use mittens or tongs to keep yourself safe
- Refrain yourself from using charcoal infused alongside starter fluid as it might bring a very unpleasant odor to your food
- Always make sure to start off with a small amount of wood and keep adding them as you cook.
- Don't be afraid to experiment with different types of wood for newer flavor and experiences.
- Always keep a notebook near you and note jot down whatever you are doing or learning and use them during the future session. This will help you to evolve and move forward.

THE CORE ELEMENTS OF SMOKING

Smoking is a very indirect method of cooking that relies on a number of different factors to give you the most perfectly cooked meal that you are looking for. Each of these components is very important to the whole process as they all work together to create the meal of your dreams.

- **Time**: Unlike grilling or even Barbequing, smoking takes a really long time and requires a whole lot of patience. It takes time for the smoky flavor to slowly get infused into the meats. Jus to bring things into comparison, it takes an about 8 minutes to fully cook a steak through direct heating, while smoking (indirect heating) will take around 35-40 minutes.

- **Temperature:** When it comes to smoking, the temperature is affected by a lot of different factors that are not only limited to the wind, cold air temperatures but also the cooking wood's dryness. Some smokers work best with large fires that are controlled by the draw of a chimney and restricted airflow through the various vents of the cooking chamber and firebox. While other smokers tend to require smaller fire with fewer coals as well as a completely different combination of the vent and draw controls. However, most smokers are designed to work at temperatures as low as 180 degrees Fahrenheit to as high as 300 degrees Fahrenheit. But the recommend temperature usually falls between 250 degrees Fahrenheit and 275 degrees Fahrenheit.

- **Airflow:** The level of air to which the fire is exposed to greatly determines how your fire will burn and how quickly it will burn the fuel. For instance, if you restrict air flow into the firebox by closing up the available vents, then the fire will burn at a low temperature and vice versa. Typically in smokers, after lighting up the fire, the vents are opened to allow for maximum air flow and is then adjusted throughout the cooking process to make sure that optimum flame is achieved.

- **Insulation:** Insulation is also very important when it comes to smokers as it helps to easily manage the cooking process throughout the whole cooking session. A good insulation allows smokers to efficiently reach the desired temperature instead of waiting for hours upon hours!

CONCLUSION

I can't express how honored I am to think that you found my book interesting and informative enough to read it all through to the end. I thank you again for purchasing this book and I hope that you had as much fun reading it as I had writing it. I bid you farewell and encourage you to move forward and find your true Smoked Meat spirit!

GET YOUR FREE GIFT

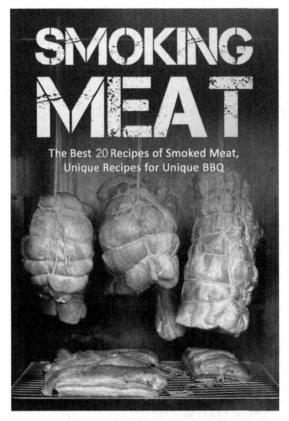

Subscribe to our Mail List and get your FREE copy of the book

'Smoking Meat: The Best 20 Recipes of Smoked Meat, Unique Recipes for Unique BBQ'

https://tiny.cc/smoke20

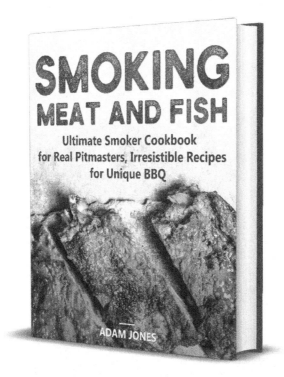

https://www.amazon.com/dp/B08B39QL1J

https://www.amazon.com/dp/B095BVWK21

https://www.amazon.com/dp/B08L54RVHH

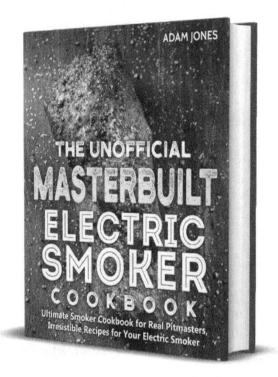

https://www.amazon.com/dp/1098708040

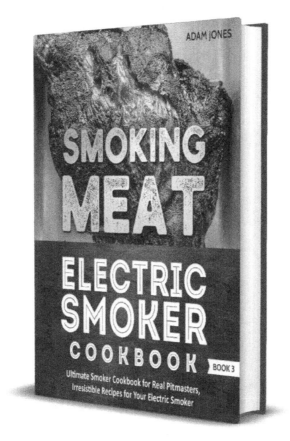

https://www.amazon.com/dp/1790483328

https://www.amazon.com/dp/1696175380

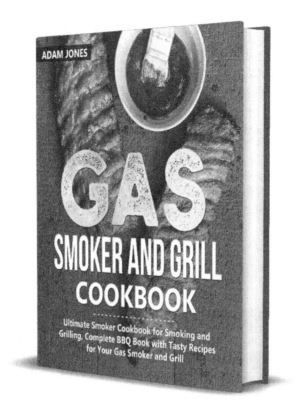

https://www.amazon.com/dp/1703307216

P.S. Thank you for reading this book. If you've enjoyed this book, please don't shy, drop me a line, leave a review or both on Amazon. I love reading reviews and your opinion is extremely important for me.

My Amazon page: www.amazon.com/author/adjones

WOOD PELLET SMOKER AND GRILL COOKBOOK

The Ultimate Barbecue Cookbook for Smoking and Grilling Irresistible Meat, Poultry, Fish, Vegetable, Game Recipes

ADAM JONES